Tea Tent, Agafay, Morocco

Trevor and Kwan-Shik south of Marrakesh, Morocco

ROAD TRIPS

ROAD TRIPS
Journeys in the Unspoiled World

Trevor Carolan

Mother Tongue Publishing Limited
Salt Spring Island, BC
Canada

MOTHER TONGUE PUBLISHING LIMITED
290 Fulford-Ganges Road, Salt Spring Island, B.C. V8K 2K6 Canada
www.mothertonguepublishing.com
Represented in North America by Heritage Group Distribution.

Book Design by Mark Hand.
Cover Image Credit: johnwoodcock (iStock)
All Photos courtesy of Kwan-Shik Kwon
Printed on Antique Natural, FSC-Recycled.
Printed and bound in Canada.

Mother Tongue Publishing acknowledges the assistance of the Province of British Columbia through the B.C. Arts Council. We acknowledge the support of the Canada Council for the Arts. Nous remercions le Conseil des arts du Canada de son soutien.

Canada Council for the Arts | Conseil des arts du Canada

LIBRARY AND ARCHIVES CANADA CATALOGUING IN PUBLICATION
Title: Road trips : journeys in the unspoiled world / Trevor Carolan.
Names: Carolan, Trevor, author.
Identifiers: Canadiana (print) 20200209825 | Canadiana (ebook) 20200209965 | ISBN 9781896949802 (softcover) | ISBN 9781896949819 (PDF)
Subjects: LCSH: Carolan, Trevor—Travel. | LCSH: Voyages around the world. | CSH: Creative nonfiction, Canadian (English) | CSH: Travelers' writings, Canadian (English) | LCGFT: Creative nonfiction. | LCGFT: Travel writing.
Classification: LCC G465 .C37 2020 | DDC 910.4/1—dc23

MIX
Paper from responsible sources
FSC® C103567
FSC www.fsc.org

For Patrick, Erin, and Ailish

Always the heart

There are two kinds of simplicity, the simplicity of going away and the simplicity of return. The last is the ultimate in sophistication.

Patrick Kavanagh

Not all places are meant to be found…not all times are right for the finding. Sometimes what you find will not be what you sought…sometimes you will find what cannot be looked for.

Patricia Monaghan

Contents

INTRODUCTION—*12*

Marrakesh Blues MOROCCO—*14*

Meeting a French Artist in Bali INDONESIA—*21*

Coming Home to the Lotus Sutra INDIA—*27*

San Francisco, of the Sacred and Profane CALIFORNIA—*33*

Down Lighthouse Lane JAMAICA—*42*

Lisbon's Iberian Soul PORTUGAL—*48*

A Desert Mantra ARIZONA—*58*

Cuba, Fidel, and Che: Hasta la Victoria, Siempre! CUBA—*62*

Wrestling with Time JAPAN AND BRITISH COLUMBIA—*77*

La France Toujours La France FRANCE—*81*

The Paradise Variations HAWAII—*105*

The River to Tir Na Nóg IRELAND—*107*

Dance Your Prayers SQUAMISH BACKCOUNTRY, BRITISH COLUMBIA—*125*

Grooving in the Higher Heights NEPAL—*129*

Chandernagore WEST BENGAL—*138*

In Poland *Dzien Dobry* Means Aloha POLAND—*142*

Living the Artist's Life in Madrid SPAIN—*158*

Where Three Dreams Cross COAST RANGE, BRITISH COLUMBIA—*172*

Dusk Along the Mekong LAOS—*175*

ACKNOWLEDGEMENTS—*195*

ABOUT THE AUTHOR—*196*

INTRODUCTION

They say write what you love. I have always loved travelling, and when I'm not on the road, I take pleasure in reading about the travels of others. Travel tales have been with us since the days of Herodotus. A Greek historian and scribe, he loved sharing details of the places and people he encountered around the ancient world. He understood that with storytelling, the older things are, the newer the wisdom we find in them. It's how you tell the tale.

Travel writing allows readers to shift gears to another place and time, filling their senses even in an armchair with news of the details that make life worth living. Effective travel reporting captures the world and makes us want to be part of the story. Often, critical decisions are involved—and consequences. Travelling, unlike holiday-making, can be like standing at the corner of Mindfulness Avenue and the Boulevard of Broken Dreams. Which way now? What comes next? You pay to learn.

Veteran travellers know that the secret to a smooth journey lies in preparation, and that good fortune is best repaid with courtesy and restraint. You remain grateful for the small gifts of the road. Locals recognize that the only outsiders who are truly gleeful, and shouting about it, are fresh off the boat, drunk, or haven't had the mosquito bites and diarrhoea yet. Good judgement comes from experience.

Travel is a chance to see and learn, to wipe the slate clean and try new things. If living well is the best revenge, there aren't many better ways to prove that than travel. A meaningful journey gives us the opportunity to get away and reimagine ourselves and our possibilities, to encounter the sacred and sublime, to be healed and return whole.

On the road, the best way to cultivate a deeper sense of a destination is to walk through and around it. Nothing else offers the immediacy and fine detail of walking and carefully observing. Walking slow is the Tai Chi of learning about new cultures and peoples. There's plenty of walking in the stories that follow.

Travel is about exploration, about experiencing the human and physical ecologies of a place that makes it unique and worth sharing, what the Taoist master Lao-tzu called "the ten thousand things." Good travel reporting recalls remarkable landscapes, intriguing peoples, and encounters with art, music, history, architecture, food and wine, literature, cultural signifiers. These are the basic elements in *Road Trips*.

Travellers have long known that their journey is at least as important as the destination, and that like preparation, timing is everything. Pandemics, natural disasters, or unhealthy political climates can mitigate against adventuring, and an easy chair and a good book of travel tales always make an ideal complement to a cozy fire or a restful summer's day when the wisdom of caution, frugality, or the comfort of home may be uppermost.

During many of these journeys that follow, I am joined by my wife, Kwan-shik. Whether haggling in bazaars, navigating hotel and flight routes online and off, or choosing the right roadside eating stall, her patience, humour, street smarts, and Korean bodyguard character have paid off time and time again. It's good to share company on the road.

Happy trails and happy reading. As Socrates had it, may you count the wise to be the wealthy, and may your travels be blessed. Peace under heaven...

Trevor Carolan
North Vancouver, 2020

MARRAKESH BLUES

MOROCCO

I'd been thinking about the Sahara for a while.
A book on my shelf kept reminding me—Peter Mayne's *A Year in Marrakesh.* We found it thirty years ago in the Himalayas near Pokhara, and I've always attributed my recovery from paratyphoid fever there to clean well water, that book, and the village barber's superb red opium. It was costly, but for fifty Nepali rupees and my copy of Jack Kerouac's *The Town and the City* that a Gurkha shopkeeper took in trade, it was a fair deal and left me enough for a last visit to the barber.

I read Mayne's account in the dreamy cloud you get from long recuperative days on the *O,* half-asleep, half-awake. An Englishman, he departed India after partition and repaired to Morocco in 1950. His portrait of the red desert city is enticing. I'd also read Paul Bowles, who wrote about Morocco for decades after taking Gertrude Stein's advice that he settle there. Bowles fixed on Tangier's "international zone," an out-of-time, autonomous city-state that William Burroughs fled to, seeking cheap living, hashish, Arab rent boys, and the stinging solitude that creeps in from the *bled*, the arid world beyond. Mayne writes from another vantage of the world. He mastered the language, got thick with the locals, and found his story in the crowded *souks* of Marrakesh, with its almost medieval Medina quarters on the edge of the Sahara.

A French translation opportunity arose for a book I'd done on one of the Beats, and I had reason to cross the Atlantic with my wife, Kwan-shik. The Pompidou in Paris had recently featured a major exhibition: Beat Paris, Beat L.A., Beat Art, you name it. Nobody does these things quite like the French. They're invested in the Beats: Ferlinghetti earned his doctorate at the Sorbonne; Ginsberg, Corso, and Burroughs all holed up in Paris to write and live there on the cheap at Rue Git-le-Coeur, across from Nôtre-Dame; Kerouac stayed long enough to crank out a draft of his *Satori in Paris;* and always there is the occult creativity of Brion Gysin, that odd surrealist painter-savant who Canada has never really claimed as its own.

Patching up the pinhole leaks in my travelling shoes, and gluing in pads against blisters, I watched with gratitude one evening as Kwan-shik mended my new travelling sweater, bought cheap at a Thrift Shop, in almost exactly the right shade of green, and covered its company logo with an unused school crest from years ago. With my backpack ready for zipping up, I remembered a thin pair of wool gloves and a scarf—just in case—and my telescope umbrella with its tight wooden knob for dark nights or bad dogs.

"You're coming to France for the Ginsberg book?" Justine, our painter friend in the 6th arrondissement in Paris asked. "Then why not go to Maroc? I tell you where to stay..."

We packed for Morocco through the morning in Lisbon, drinking coffee and munching custard *natas.* It's good to get back your sea legs in Portugal after long flights. The architecture is memorable; people are friendly, the food is excellent. You tram to Alfama, the hilly old Moorish quarter to hear the fado singers, the women wailing their *saudad*e in black shawls, musicians playing on metabolic scales, the chilled green wine, pork and clams, octopus.

In Marrakesh you can stay in backpack dives for chump change, or chill out upscale for sixty dollars a night in Gueliz district hotels in the *nouvelle ville* beyond the historic medina walls. French artists have loved Marrakesh since the painter Jacques Majorelle settled here in the 1920s to build his grand botanical garden. Mayne's book remains a serviceable guide; he wrote daily at the Café de France a few minutes from

Katoubia Mosque and both are central landmarks. All that's required is a free city map from the airport, which is modern, efficient, and feels secure. Women workers wear head scarves like my mother used to wear to Sunday mass, and there are photographs of the king, Mohammed VI, on the walls. Regarded as a reformer, he's usually smiling and people are affectionate towards him. Morocco is unexpectedly contemporary; young woman outside are remarkably stylish in leggings, smart sandals, and *nijab* in strikingly attractive colours; others simply go uncovered. You're not far from Europe after all. The oasis greenery is surprisingly rich, like its desert birdlife.

You're in North Africa now: the minarets, the call to prayer. *Hamdullilah*. On the boulevards outside it feels as if you haven't shaved for a couple of days; always there's a little grit under your nails.

This is a place of curious dreams. Coffee and clouds of strong tobacco everywhere. We adopt the Diamant Vert off Rue Ibn Hamza as our breakfast place. At our first visit, I switch to drinking *thé* du menthe without rock sugar. The coffee is short and bitter.

The Medina is the old, foreign legion-style city with pockmarked walls of red brick. We hire a horse-cart taxi, and the cabbie relates the holes are for nesting birds—migrating sparrows, pigeons, blackbirds: "We Marrakeshis love our birds," he chuckles. I recall that pigeon pie is a specialty here: in the desert, there is no superfluity; every last thing has a purpose.

In the dry lands a melodious yellow warbler arcs past, followed by a precise swerve of white speedy terns. Playing Tai Chi in the garden at six AM, I see mottled finches flit and jostle each other aggressively to drink from a pool. Soaring above us, a fine dark hawk.

In the *bled* where the countryside morphs to stony desert, lines of camels amble down hard baked trails. A few have riding saddles. Grey, fuzzy newborns pronk stiff-legged like wonky gazelles, leaning in at water groves among olive trees, palms, and thorny bush. Nearby, the men look on in their *djellabas*. Every compact village crammed in a shady canyon has its pair of mosques; most now seem to use recorded calls. The chunter of grazing sheep, crickets, and the chatter of desert songbirds carries on the bone-dry air.

A friend sends a letter. I write in reply:

> Marrakesh is a red city, ochre adobe-covered baked brick walls; convivial, bustling. Early mornings are pleasantly cool. The Djemma el Fna, a great public square, is frantic at night with throngs of people milling about, fires blazing around the edges near restaurants and the bazaar stalls that sell delicious sheep's head stew. Wild gnoussa mountain drummers and horn men who wail on shams—those that Brion Gysin alleged in the Fifties are the vestigial Pan-pipers of ancient Hellas—arrive at dusk when the snake-charmers leave. It's still all here. Last night, a blue-black desert man flayed hypnotic trance notes, over and over on his two-stringed goatskin gurmi with drummers and cymbalists circled around him, same note after plangent note, building wave on wave of repetitive desert sounds in the dark as old village men and slick-dressed hipster dudes broke down and danced uncontrollably. I said, "This is wilder than Jimi Hendrix in '68," then flashed that he'd been here too, immersing himself in the trance after Brian Jones from The Stones had pointed the way, and after crazy Gysin from Edmonton before him had turned on the London intelligentsia to the desert vibrations. Crowds gathered round called out "Sa-har, Sa-har..." Later, we wandered through the Mellah, the dwindling Jewish quarter; still a few Stars of David set in the walls. Thought of you and your family.

We hire a Jeep to take us into the Atlas Mountains. South of the city where things turn dry quickly, Ali our Berber driver veers off the road and pounds across rugged country. "I will take you where no tourist ever goes," he says, hammering the motor along a terrifying precipice cut above a sheer-drop gorge of great height. We are in a mystic landscape, ashen with fear. Ali relishes our terror. Finally, we emerge from the chasm and surge higher yet into the Atlas with a massive white range of peaks behind us.

In the mountains, Berber men leave to work in the cities; women stay at home harvesting wild foods, weaving rugs from their sheep's wool, and harvest healing *argan* oil from the berries of a tree in the olive family. At a women's cooperative, we buy a pot of their unguent mixed with red thyme. There's a comforting herbal buzz when I rub it in at evening time. Argan grows only in this place in southern Morocco, and the King encourages villagers to plant trees against desertification.

A day later we mount camels. The males are bad-tempered beasts with an attitude. You roll along, wobbly with the flow, seated on a hard platform. You're higher than you'd expect and had better not fall; steadily, the appalling smell of camel seeps into every rag you own. But it's a simple life, the desert. The nomads say, in French, that they live in paradise.

Driving on, we aim for the caravan trails across the dunes. Ali takes us out to an oasis hamlet with its herds of sheep, donkeys, tough quiet shepherds, nomad tents, the lot.

I ask in a scrabble of French, "What does 'Sahara' mean in your language?"

Ali looks at the endless rolling hills and dunes, laughs with a Berber friend, and responds: "Emptiness… "

"He sounds like the Dalai Lama," Kwan-shik says in agreement.

Moving south we hail upon a cluster of black homespun woollen tents stretched horizontally with ropes five or six feet above ground on wooden poles, the ubiquitous dwellings of semi-nomadic herders. In these well-used tents, you sit on knotted brightly dyed carpets. For a few dirhams the locals serve hot mint tea in thimble glasses with a little pot of argan honey and torn bits of flatbread. With a local man as guide, we set off trekking across the undulating dunes. Within fifteen minutes, we lose track of every landmark but the distant mountains. After another hour in the heat and flying desert bugs, we come upon an abandoned *riad*, a walled family compound of stone and adobe. We rest in its shade. "Do you like it?" Ali asks.

"Why is it abandoned? No water?"

"You can buy this riad. You and me can make a business," he tells us. "With two hectares of land, 35,000 euros."

Fifty grand for a ruin with a marginal blip of the Sahara desert? Ridiculous. So why am I thinking it over? We haven't seen a deal like this in Vancouver since the Liberal party and the condo kings sold out the city to Big Time Operators. "Europeans buy them," Ali continues. "We can fix it up for a spa hotel." I wonder where Ali got his training as a wilderness guide—the Chamber of Commerce?

Another day we sight a line of white polythene structures on the horizon. Greenhouses? "No," Ali explains, "modern tents for tourists to experience a night in the desert. They build fires, sing and dance, gaze at the stars."

Another version of the authentic experience. Then a second letter, this from a young writer:

> Sitting in a coffeeshop in Tofino, snaking some wifi. Came up to rest from the city. The sun came out today; squads of Aussie and German backpackers are arriving. I've been hiking the rainforest figuring out my next moves and taking in the west coast's natural beauty. This is a tourist town. Pretty girls tell you how "they'd hate to see you disappointed if you didn't make a deposit on this once-in-a-lifetime opportunity to see grizzly bears in their natural habitat." White dreadlocked guys talk about how they're "living for the surf" and huck their empty beer cans.

You can find or lose yourself along the Sahara's edge, no problem. I've seen now what Gysin, Bowles, and the Beat innovators were intrigued by here. Morocco is a bumpy, fascinating land. Hopefully, it won't be invaded by the usual suspects whenever an Arab nation starts to get ahead. We meet Didier, a Frenchman in the trucking business, hauling produce and leather goods to Europe. He confirms the economy is thriving, is cheerful too about the new French president, Macron. "He's well educated and loves poetry," he claims. "You'd be surprised. From memory he can recite fifty lines of Baudelaire."

I ask if he knows those writers who travelled between Maroc and Paris in the fifties, but the American names mean nothing to him. "However," he says, "there are still Europeans coming down here to go crazy…"

Some things never change. One morning we say *au revoir* to the waiters at Diamond Vert, to the grocery boys down Avenue Abdelkarim who never cheat you. Everyone smiles, a little sad to say goodbye. Only after we return home and watch *Lawrence of Arabia* on Netflix, do I realize the bedouin tents in the film are precisely like those we stayed in beneath the Atlas. Truly, the way is endless…

2018

MEETING A FRENCH ARTIST IN BALI

INDONESIA

Prior to another long Asian journey, I am at home, packing up. My mother calls to remind me that a documentary on The Chieftains, Ireland's great traditional music ensemble, is on television. I flick on the program. At one point, the acclaimed late-Ulster harpist Derek Bell, remarks on what he discovered through music, observing mystically that, "Lord Shiva says, 'First of all, learn what it is you want to do, then you will have learned what it is that you like.'"

I like travelling and writing. On a Friday afternoon in January, I depart with Kwan-shik for Bali. The route is awkward, five separate flights—San Francisco, Shanghai, Hong Kong, Singapore, Denpasar. Wearily, I recall that Captain Cook and his men took three years to reach these waters under sail. It could be worse.

Kwan-shik has arranged by Internet to have a driver meet us at the airport when we land. It's a handy arrangement. We make our way without incident through Denpasar and the sweltering night in Ngyomen's Japanese micro-van. He will take us to Sanur, ten miles away from the Babylon tourist scene at Kuta Beach where, only a few years ago, two hundred Australians and other foreigners were murdered in a horrific disco bombing by Islamic terrorists. En route we pass the familiar scene of third-world night-market stalls, open-air noodle soup vendors, and shops lit by the customary single bare light bulb. The charcoal scent of cooking fires drifts in through the open windows.

We settle into a compact guesthouse in Sanur run by a veteran Australian pair; the eight small bungalows are situated on an airy winding road lined with shop-front businesses along both sides. It's a walled compound with plenty of lush vegetation and a neat, small pool tiled cobalt blue, with a couple of benches for cooling off and stretching out. Our bungalow has a fan, small fridge for cold water and fruit, and an attached shower room built of stone. Incense and mosquito coil are already burning as we haul our cases in. We've had a long journey. Shaking off the road dust, we crash early in the sultry heat.

Breakfast is excellent local coffee, fruit, and toasted bread served on a deep-covered teak veranda out front. The owners chat easily with guests, and we meet a Dutch couple who journey to Bali every year. The atmosphere is informal; the jokes are in good fun. We arrange to join the Hollanders next day for a journey to the north of the island, about ninety kilometres through the mountains.

From there we set off *jalan-jalan,* walking-walking in Bahasa, knocking about the village that stretches along the road, passing restaurants large and small, clothing shops, internet cafés, a mix of boutiques and various guest houses. We browse about, comparing costs with the public market, just beginning to open in the day's early heat. Progressing further, we pass a large temple constructed of plastered sun-baked bricks. Once the plaster has fallen away, everything looks old and weathered. But flowers and small offerings of petals and rice on banana leaf are left everywhere and in front of every shop; incense burns, mixing with the unmistakable smell of vegetable decay in tropic heat.

We're back in Asia.

The edginess hasn't really disappeared since the Islamic bombings, so we avoid crowds. The reduced trade has local sellers and transport drivers constantly nagging outsiders for business. and this becomes debilitating, taking away from the beauty of Bali's superb natural landscapes.

We follow a long road down to the beach and emerge where the street ends upon a small gathering of food hawkers. Our first day's beach lunch is fish-ball noodle soup and satay chicken, 30,000 rupiah, about three dollars. We are helped in changing our money by a young Frenchman from Lyons. He has a local wife and child and in a patois of English and French explains that they are working on a way for him to stay here. We meander back along the water. Sanur isn't a great beach; the sand is a little unkempt, crabbed with stone or coral, and the water is full of seaweed, but we get wet and enjoy the sun between drifts of heavy cloud.

Along the beach there is a small temple where cremations are held. Bali people are, for the most part, still chiefly Hindu. The burning site is recently charred.

We come upon a new word used to describe people like ourselves—"flashpackers." A spin on the old backpacker lifestyle we've followed for decades. It suggests a newer version of ourselves that wants a bit more comfort—a room in reasonably cheap local digs, but with a shower and toilet of one kind or another.

Komang, the girl who looks after the veranda for breakfast each day, is lovely. Her conversation is pleasurable and upbeat, filled with cultural reference points from life on the island. She tells us over cinnamon coffee what qualities the Balinese regard as being attractive in a girl: "But what's especially important," I ask? She answers, "*Chantique*...to be beautiful and simple."

Several days after this, we find ourselves taking coffee and sweets one evening in a café called Chantique.

With the Dutch couple from Rotterdam, we set off north, their driver negotiating us through village rice fields. Bali is near the equator, so there are only minor seasonal differences through the year and rice grows year-round. With its regular tropical rains, the fields are a quilt of vivid greens and shimmery ponds. Flocks of ducks devour the insects that would eat the rice plants, rounding out the symbiotic nature of the fields with their narrow raised dykes that frequently give way to terraced steps. There are flocks everywhere. Over the ages, the fields themselves have been ploughed perfectly horizontal to accommodate the *sawah,* wet rice culture.

Driving on through deep country, we pass village processions—local groups honouring the Bali calendar's many sacred festivals with flower garlands and trays of fruit; the participants dressed in their finest glimmery sarongs and carrying holy tee umbrellas, with gamelan gongs and hand drums. Driving into higher territory, we come to Candikuning, a lake with a temple complex where another procession is setting off just as we arrive, and where a funeral procession will pass us heading in the other direction a short time later. People here seem to drop what they're doing and pick up on the ceremonies spontaneously. Ritual is an intrinsic part of everyday life.

Above Lake Bratan we stop to buy local fruit from a roadside stall, mangosteens and rambutans, and monkeys emerge from the dense bush, arguing among themselves while they beg for food. Carrying on through the mountains with breathtaking views of hillside rice terraces, we come to the coffee-growing area around Munduk. The driver recommends we stop for lunch at a restaurant and coffee-roastery on a high peak before carrying on to the North Bali coast. The terrain is like Darjeeling in the Himalayan foothills. Coffee-planting makes sense here in the same way that tea does there.

It's evident as we push further that the decline in tourism since the bombings has hit the north coast hard. Life looks leaner in the villages.

I've learned of a rare Buddhist monastery here, so we stop to visit the Brahma Vihar Arama. The temple is kept in tidy condition with its several meditation halls and a quiet, restful garden. I am struck by a quote from the *Kalama Sutra*, the Discourse upon the Encouragement of Free Inquiry, that is posted for general perusal—"Study and Learn" it recommends.

We take another day of rest at Sanur to enjoy the sun then journey on to Ubud in the hills. A funky town set amid vivid green rice fields and jungle streams. Hot and sunny. After the initial crush of the town core, we find a place to stay that proves something like an old Rajah's palace with lush water gardens, cool breezy rooms, and lovely views of the fields, birds, and butterflies.

From my travel notes: "it's a splurge but I book in for Kwan-shik's sake, for putting up with me through thick and thin all these years."

In the pool later, after meditation and Tai Chi, I am wading in the cool water and observing the slow ebb and flow of life in the rice fields beyond. One of the guesthouse girls arrives with flowers for the garden shrine, offering incense and sprinkling water on the shrine stone with elaborate, delicate gestures of her hands. Wonderful stillness. A short time later, a tall quiet woman, Western, wearing a broad sun hat, descends through the garden by the shady water and also begins playing Tai Chi. Not many Westerners take the time to really learn, but she knows what she is doing. Later, I mention her to Kwan-shik.

The following morning, the scene repeats itself. After practicing her Tai Chi, the woman sets up a paint box and easel, working with watercolours. It would be ungracious to disturb her, but twenty minutes later, Kwan-shik arrives with coffee and after a few minutes strikes up conversation with the painter in the straw hat. They talk a while, and Kwan-shik gestures me over for a look. The watercolour is of the garden, quickly done, capturing the vitality of the tropic growth. It's atmospheric work.

Justine, we learn, is a sculptor and painter visiting from Paris with a friend. We look at her sketchbook: her watercolour studies of the old Singapore shop-houses she encountered on the way are excellent. It's a shame our paths won't cross here for much longer.

It feels a little like Somerset Maugham in the tropics, but with the thought that one day we might collaborate on something from our respective notebooks, and as travellers have done since Roman times, we exchange addresses. I remember that in my case there is something perhaps of interest, an essay I've recently published on Leonard Cohen's last poetry. A kind of writer's calling card. We carry them about like Johnny Appleseed. Worth a look?

"D'accord..."

It's not a bad policy. Before much time passes, we'll meet again in France, then Hong Kong en route from India. Justine will stay with us in Vancouver on her way to a mask-carving sojourn on Pender Island. At the premiere in Brussels of my documentary film, *Cascadia: The Life and Breath of the World,* the opening image of our Blue Planet will be one of hers. At the centenary of the Battle of the Somme, we'll bow our heads together in gratitude, and then walk the slopes at Vimy Ridge in awe of Walter Allward's Michelangelo-like limestone national memorial.

In Canada, our children will mature and set off on travels of their own. We'll check on the French elections and plan a retreat in a village near the border with Spain. Justine will build herself a new studio in the countryside and make nettle soup when we arrive. We notice that her *atelier* sign on the winding village road out of Sainte Jeanne d'Arc reads "Studio Chantique."

2002-2019

COMING HOME TO THE LOTUS SUTRA

INDIA

Some journeys feel as if they were forever ago. Others remain vividly in mind, from our awareness at the time, when our ears and eyes, our heart, were fully attentive. Recently, while preparing a journey to India to gather an anthology of contemporary stories from South Asia for college readers, I was heartened that Kwan-shik could come too. We wanted to see Mother India again. Organically, the cue cards began slipping into place.

As our departure neared, reports grew of political instability throughout South Asia and flashed on the news. I grew apprehensive. Even finalizing a workable itinerary on budget was unusually problematic. Kwan-shik brought a bag of fortune cookies home one evening though, and immediately we began receiving more positive signals: "You are Heading in the Right Direction," "You and Your Partner Will Soon Experience Great Happiness," "You Are Heading for a Land of Sunshine and Fun." Things were looking up.

Shortly before departing, an article attracted my attention. Writing on Korean Buddhism, Robert Buswell reported that travel has always been "an integral part of Buddhism since its very inception." Devotion and missionary pilgrimage, he suggests, evolve directly from India's ancient indigenous *śramana* tradition of itinerant wandering. "Initiation into that ascetic life was termed a 'going forth,'" he says. "We might today call this a 'setting out' on a journey of personal discovery." That gave me heart. What had my anxieties been all about? Suddenly, our upcoming journey had a higher purpose. Besides, I had old dharma business that needed settling.

When Hong Kong's stupendous skyline loomed ahead, it felt good to touch down again in Confucian lands. Outside, the old colony's Dragon Peaks sulked in dreary mist. While we transferred between flights, I heard announcements for Siem Reap, Kuala Lumpur, Bangkok, Singapore. Different geography, different environment here. Signs on escalators and moving stairways read: Take Care of the Children and Elderly.

Ready for the onward leg to Kolkata, formerly Calcutta, I looked about. Expatriate businessmen leaned against walls talking on cell phones. Young Indian women lounged in jewelled footwear. When the boarding gate opened, the predictable Asian crush for seats erupted. Travel light.

During a stretch break at the rear of the plane, I met an Englishman flying back to India from a sidebar visit to Vietnam. The number of huge newly built Christian churches he saw there was astonishing, he said. Now he was heading back to India for two months, having his teeth fixed at Goa for a fraction of the cost in London.

"I've noticed there seems to be rekindled interest in pilgrimages and long-stay journeys in India," he reckoned. "A reaction to mass tourism, I think. Look at Thailand. It's overrun with backpackers nowadays. India still frightens 'em a bit. Depends what you're after, doesn't it?"

In Kolkata we headed for Ballygunge to stay with old friends. Outside our taxi window, the eternal road-sweepers were hard at it, labouring in the dust. New office blocks already looked worn in the heat. Soon the first slum hovels appeared, propped against alley walls. Then came the ditches, the rooting pigs, and tropical stinks, on and on. Back again to Mother India.

But we're on a sentimental journey this time. First, catch up with friends and talk and talk. Tomorrow there'll be the countryside beyond the temples at Dakineshwar and Belur Math, out to the old French colony at Chandernagore on the Hooghly River. What I wanted most to see in Kolkata was the little temple at Dakuria Lake where, nearly forty years ago, as a young trekker I'd first encountered Buddhism in a living way. Staying with the same Bengali friends we were visiting now, I'd set off wandering one morning and heard a voice from behind ask, "Do you know the way to the Japan Temple?"

Turning, I'd seen a pilgrim monk clad in a simple umber robe, travelling on foot to the sacred places of the Buddha Life—shaved head, flip-flop sandals, thin shoulder sack, and a walking stick. He'd walked like this, he explained, all the way from southern Thailand, through Burma, and civil war-ravaged Bangladesh. Originally German, he had discovered the dharma from books where he'd worked mining opals in the Australian outback after WWII. He took his vows at a Thai forest *wat*.

I didn't know the Japan Temple, but said I'd enjoy helping him find it, so we strolled together for hours. Then we heard a booming from across a lake. The monk's ears picked up at the sound, and we stepped lively, arriving upon a little white-and-red temple where the monk hoped to stay.

The monk whispered, "Follow me." I copied what he did. We entered up the temple steps, bowed to a Buddha image on a small altar, and took places on the floor among a group of worshippers, mostly women, in fading light. The repetitive chanting came easily enough, *Na-Mu Myo-Ho Ren-Ge Kyo*... As my confidence grew, I fell into the *puja* action with the swaying motion of those around me. The chant was completely absorbing, and over and over the thunder of a mighty dharma drum had the whole temple ringing. The Japanese monks took turns hammering at it like *taiko* masters. Darkness fell long before I left with a silent nod to the wandering monk. I returned home with a ringing in my head and in my heart. Without looking for it, I think it was there that I first experienced, briefly, something like selflessness. Maybe the dharma had been looking for me. Years passed, but I never forgot the Japan Temple.

Passing the roadside sweepers, I recalled that Indian Buddhists these days are largely Ambedkarite, converts from the Dalit community long stigmatized through caste restrictions. Fed up with Untouchability, they became Buddhists in the millions under Dr. Ambedkar in the 1940s and '50s. The mass conversions breathed life into India's dormant Buddhism. Plenty of confusion arose at the time, and the new dharma followers were short of proper teachers. Tibetans lent a hand. So did Japanese Nichiren monks who had established a small Calcutta temple devoted to the Lotus Sutra—my first dharma home. The lake area has since been renamed Rabindra Sarovar.

At times, Kolkata feels like a city verging on eco-cide—unbreathable air, grinding traffic, poverty. Yet people find tranquility in their contained neighbourhood worlds. The blue-tiled address of our friends welcomed us to the shady alleys of Ballygunge. Upstairs in a dim interior hung a remarkable painting in Ellora Cave-style of the *Padma-pani* image, *The Buddha Holds the Lotus in His Hand.* Large and gentle, it's a quintessentially Indian visualization. Our friend, Uma, created this... *the Jewel in the Lotus.*

At dinner we caught up on old times. Retired banker and elder brother Sam talked about Guru-Chela, the archetypal Indian learning relationship between Master-Disciple. Sam offered what he feels is a better translation: *Guru-Shishya.* It's new to me. "The Guru"—in Chinese it's *Sifu/Shifu*—"creates the stimulus to learn more," Sam says. "It's an individualized condition for learning."

"We have cosmetic surgery for the exterior. Indian yogic practice is a way of remaking the interior, the mind. That's the next level."

Almost immediately in my readings of Indian newspapers, I notice Guru-Shishya crop up. There's no replacing local knowledge.

Beside me on the table sat a bottle of green salsa: "Druk Mustard Sauce Product of Bhutan." I studied the label, reflecting that even the little Shangri-la of Gross National Happiness has export considerations nowadays. There's globalization for you! And it tastes good, not fiery. Outside, distant *pujas* were underway—someone blew a conch, then the chants and metallic jangling of triangles rose from little Hindu temples. The alley below was empty, serene in moonlight.

Meanwhile, Calcutta has its history—the Armenian Ghats, the ancient Portuguese settlement at Bandol Church, Victoria Memorial, and a new Mother Theresa mural at Kalighat metro station near the city's holiest Hindu temple. It all makes sense. What doesn't is the nightmare traffic gridlock. Yet there are far fewer beggars now.

India, media mavens tell us constantly, is the next world superpower with a 150 million citizens of certifiable economic middle-class status, roughly fifteen percent of the population. She has the atomic bomb and an educated and influential worldwide diaspora. Dalits comprise another fifteen percent of the population, mostly at the bottom, but giddy Western reports seldom note this anymore. Apart from terrorism, it's the call centres and outsource operations in Bangalore—India's most recognizably with-it city—that feature attention. India is still a country of extremes, subject to the biases of other peoples' measurements.

No suffering, no enlightenment. At last we set off for Japan Temple. It's not as easy to find as it once was; tall buildings have sprung up all around. My heart danced a little at the sight—an oasis in a crowded city, gleaming white and red-trimmed within a walled compound and a front garden. After nearly forty years, I was back like the prodigal son. A monk sat having tea with visitors from Japan when we arrived, and luckily he spoke some English. Master Asai smiled at my situation.

He led us to the prayer hall. I'd had a dread of this—wondering if what was unforgettable for so long might somehow now appear gaudy, too much of this or that. Lotus Sutra devotions receive a mixed welcome in North America anyway, often dismissed as a way for flaky L.A. types to chant for a new Mercedes, although I hear that Afro-Americans seem to find it a source of refuge, and Tina Turner is an enthusiastic proponent. I've wondered if returning to this original source of what's been a repaying, worthwhile life might lead to disappointment—they say you can't go back again.

But the sense of grace remained: the same cool temple interior redolent of incense, the altar and simple Buddha image as unchanged as I remembered them. The great drum was there with its magical lettering. Everything felt, well, perfect. I looked at Kwan-shik and saw that she felt it too, the real deal. We walked about the altar slowly, like *kinhin*, walking Zen, then made our bows, rang the singing bowl three times, burned incense, made our offering.

We heard the mantra then, *Na-Mu Myo-Ho Ren-Ge Kyo*... Master Asai chanting. We joined him in the prayer, and the chant grew louder with three voices now. Soon, a new wave of devotees behind us took up, and I saw the Japanese visitors had joined us. Six voices and we chanted in unison, over and over, *Na-Mu Myo-Ho Ren-Ge Kyo*...

Master Awai deepened and threw his voice like a sounding whale.

It brought us strength and we continued. The gardener, a sun-darkened man, entered and took his seat at the drum, balancing his wooden tipper sticks in hand... *Na-Mu Myo-Ho Ren-Ge Kyo, Na-Mu Myo-Ho Ren-Ge Kyo, Na-Mu Myo-Ho Ren-Ge Kyo...* Then the dharma drum began its thunder. For decades I've carried its heavy rhythm in my head, and again it all came surging back as the drum strokes grew in power and our chanting rolled in, wave on wave. *Na-Mu Myo-Ho Ren-Ge Kyo, Na-Mu Myo-Ho Ren-Ge Kyo, Na-Mu Myo-Ho Ren-Ge Kyo...* More incense filled the hall, the temple dome became a bell, and we ourselves were ringing within it... *Na-Mu Myo-Ho Ren-Ge Kyo...*

Two high-school girls in uniform appeared from the shadows near the incense altar, joining the chant, perhaps drawn by the echo of the drum. They looked a little like the local sweepers too, and we saw that a crowd from the neighbourhood had grown around us now, everyone chanting like the first time I'd visited long ago. *Na-Mu Myo-Ho Ren-Ge Kyo, Na-Mu Myo-Ho Ren-Ge Kyo, Na-Mu Myo-Ho Ren-Ge Kyo...* We chanted and our bodies swayed with these new dharma friends, mostly Dalit and once Untouchable, as over and over, the mighty drum kept pealing out the dharma, *Na-Mu Myo-Ho Ren-Ge Kyo, Na-Mu Myo-Ho Ren-Ge Kyo, Na-Mu Myo-Ho Ren-Ge Kyo...* The tears began then, and I saw them rolling down Master Asai as well; he'd taken up a small drum himself and was striking it with tremendous spirit. We were all in it together deep in the heart of the Lotus Sutra, like a jewel arising from the dust of the world.

It was a tranquil morning, but the temple kept resonating *Na-Mu-Myo-Ho-Ren-Ge-Kyo... Na-Mu-Myo-Ho-Ren-Ge-Kyo...*

Joseph Campbell says our sacred space is where we can find ourselves again and again. India is always a tough journey, but I returned to something important in struggling Kolkata, and I've always been thankful to my unknown monk-guide there for getting it all started. In the end my book, *The Lotus Singers*, got done, and Kwan-shik and I came away with renewed love for the Lotus Sutra, every bit as cleansing, inspiring, and gratitude-inducing as the very first time I heard it.

2012

SAN FRANCISCO, OF THE SACRED AND PROFANE

CALIFORNIA

My affection for San Francisco, one of the world's great literary hub cities, spans many decades. Five years after leaving the old country and immigrating to Canada, our family headed south on a camping journey to California, and passed through the Bay City. In August 1962, we drove the thirteen-hundred-mile Pacific Coast route in my father's first car, a two-tone '54 Nash Ambassador, with the radio bopping all the way—Chubby Checker snapping "The Twist," Elvis and his irresistible "Good Luck Charm," Ray Charles crying "I Can't Stop Loving You."

In San Francisco, we experienced a memorable walkabout in "exotic" Chinatown. Awed by the towering downtown buildings, I remember crossing a busy street hearing the newspaper sellers shouting "Extra! Extra! Marilyn Monroe Found Dead!" America's sexiest sweetheart had married a local North Beach hero, Joe DiMaggio the baseball slugger, and the city was in shock.

Six years later, I returned as a young hippie after hitchhiking a thousand miles down I-5, looking for the then already mythic Summer of Love. I headed for the Fillmore Ballroom and a prophetic meeting with Bill Graham, the psychedelic rock world's first great impresario. Still in high school, but already writing for my hometown daily paper, I was commissioned by the editor to "report on the music scene in Haight-

Ashbury...tell us what it's about."

My first night in town, I walked from the YMCA through the gritty Market Street tenderloin toward the ballroom where Big Brother and the Holding Company, one of three or four iconic longhair bands of the era, were headlining. Richie Havens warmed up the crowd, along with a forgotten band from Illinois, before Big Brother's fabulous singer nearly tore the roof off the place. With a job to do, after the show I approached Graham. He was all of twenty-eight then and looked plenty older, decent, with a heavy shadow beard, and he gave me a few minutes, but he was a busy man. "Here, hang on a sec," he said, and waved over a young woman who'd been singing—sweaty and busty in loose purple trousers and strappy high heels. "This young fella's down from Vancouver working on a story. Can I introduce you to him?"

That was how I met Janis Joplin, and right off the bat she was likeable, supportive, and full of encouragement. She knew Vancouver, she said, and would love to play there with the band—could I put her in touch with a club guy that Bill knew too? I could do that, sure. "Great!" she beamed. "We'll see you up there, man. And hey, we have to get you some stories, right? Have you seen Tina Turner? She's coming back here with Ike and the band. You've *gotta* see her on Friday night. She's the greatest!" San Francisco has always been a fast ride.

That afternoon I'd called in at the enduring landmark of City Lights Books in North Beach. It held down a corner at Columbus Avenue, then as now, where Little Italy morphs seamlessly into Chinatown. I'd read Lawrence Ferlinghetti's poetry at school—"A Coney Island of the Mind," "Underwear"—there were stories in his poems you could relate to, no ancient Latin or Greek mythology needed. Making a pilgrimage to his bookstore was compulsory, and the raunchy neighbourhood with its topless bars, jazz, and old folkie hangouts exuded a seedy charm for young bucks and sailors.

By my second day in town, I was knocking around Haight-Ashbury. Still surface-colourful, it was unexpectedly rundown, and the panhandlers and stumbling casualty figures gave it an in-your-face edge. The rainbow people I'd anticipated were there, of course, but so were the religious cranks and hardcore activists. "Free Huey, here...," said one black guy in a leather jacket. "Demonstration... Join over there." You could feel the anger, but I wasn't ready for that kind of action. Bobby Kennedy and Dr. Martin Luther King, Jr. had been murdered in the previous few months, and the U.S. was in a spiritual crisis. *Peace and Love*, *Black Is Beautiful* and *Out of Vietnam Now!* bumped for attention as President Lyndon Johnson prepared to leave office and the spectre of Richard Nixon loomed from down the road in right-wing, Southern California.

The obvious out was another show at the Fillmore, and Ike and Tina Turner did not let you down with their searing rhythm and blues revue. Add Freddie King the blues guitar maestro and Blue Cheer, "the world's loudest band," named after a popular hit of acid, and the path was clear ahead. Sort of. The next Sunday, on the way to a love-in in Golden Gate Park with the Grateful Dead, I found myself grabbed by the throat with a blade tip nipping my stomach. "Gimme all your money or I'll stick ya." It was a terrifying command from a fit black dude who'd seemed okay and moved in close real fast. This was the other side of Peace and Love, the grotty poverty of San Francisco's race divides.

"Get him!" In one of the luckiest moments in my life, a strapping fellow emerged with a Doberman on a short leash. Freeing the dog, he called out hard, and my assailant broke and ran. I was in shock when my deliverer ran up and roared, "What the hell are you doing in here on your own!"

It had all happened in a blink. "You're in the wrong park! Buena Vista's full of junkies! You could have been killed." He led me out of the park directly to a police car parked unaccountably nearby. When I recovered and explained the situation, rather than giving me a sympathetic ear, the Officer Clancy type behind the wheel bellowed at me again—"Get back to the Y!" So much for frontier justice. Shaken, I didn't step outside for two days. It made a hell of a dispatch for the paper, and crossing the Golden Gate Bridge on my way back home, I retained conflicted feelings about the City by the Bay.

Geographically, San Francisco's physical setting is exceptional. Situated like Athens or Cordoba near the 38th parallel, its climate is Mediterranean. The surrounding country is dry coastal chaparral, and the productive Sonoma and Napa Valleys up the road are the heart of

California's rich wine-producing region. Southward, the splendour of the Big Sur coastal highway passes with Hispanic resonance through the historic missionary route linking Monterey, Carmel, and Santa Cruz, leading to Santa Barbara, Los Angeles, and San Diego. To the north, inland routes lead to towering redwood forests, and to the arid stock-raising and agricultural country of Ukiah and Redding. Major military and naval shipyards are housed around the Bay Area, and two major international research universities are close by at Berkeley and Stanford.

Devastated by the Great Earthquake and fire of 1906, the city sits atop the West Coast's large tectonic fault zone, and historically, its trading routes have extended northward to the Gold Rush cities: Seattle, Vancouver, and farther up to Alaska and the Yukon. The city also sits advantageously on the lucrative pan-Pacific trade routes to Japan and China, as well as to Hawaii; it long served as chief mainland entrepôt for the islands' sugar trade. As the terminus of the first U.S. transcontinental railway, the Union Pacific, completed in 1869, San Francisco grew as a transportation nexus. Upon completion of the railway, it became a magnet for Irish and Chinese migrant labourers, adding to the region's Indigenous, Hispanic, and Euro-American settlers.

What drew settlers "out West" to San Francisco was the chance to make their fortune. The city and the state have traditionally offered an opportunity to get away from social conventionality and the settled life of the U.S. East Coast. It offered space to grow. Inevitably, the city reflects the contributions of its immigrant groups: the French, whose architectural influence makes it arguably North America's most handsomely constructed major city; the Irish, whose influence on law and order, administration, sporting life, and journalism is traditional; the Chinese, whose core residential neighbourhood and commercial enterprise have attracted generations of visitors; the Italians and Portuguese whose cuisine and North Beach district have traditionally provided solace to the city's artistic and bohemian community; and the Russians, who, as refugees of the Bolshevik Revolution brought European *haute* cultural sophistication. The city has enjoyed historical links artistically and educationally with France; Gertrude and Leo Stein, Alice B. Toklas, and Isadora Duncan number among those who gravitated from the Bay City to the cultural ambiance of Paris.

San Francisco's community mosaic remained salty and uncommonly colourful. Among the attractions for Beat Generation writers and artists in the fifties were its Chinese and Japanese Buddhist temples, the Italian conviviality of North Beach, and the Irish liberality of its bars and music haunts. Like New Orleans, the city has long celebrated its sybaritic Babylon-by-the-Bay reputation, and unsurprisingly, the landmark U.S. censorship battle over Allen Ginsberg's *Howl* was fought and won here by Ginsberg and his publisher, Lawrence Ferlinghetti of City Lights Books.

Admixed has been an essentially reformist, Labour-Democratic political lineage with more than a tinge of nearby Berkeley and Stanford intellectualism. More recent San Francisco-oriented public figures have included Governor Jerry Brown, State Congressman Tom Hayden, and City Councilman Harvey Milk.

A growing interest in Zen called me back. Living on a student visa in northern California in the mid-seventies, I started hitching down to the Zen Center on Page Street. By now I was reading Allen Ginsberg and Jack Kerouac. That got me back to City Lights, to the Vesuvio bar next door, and across the bay to Berkeley. Life suddenly got more interesting. Like Calcutta, Paris, London, or New York, San Francisco had an identifiable culture, a voice, a texture. Whether this is a wave or a particle, I still can't say, but it is has been hard to keep away from its existential zing. Coffee in the morning at Caffe Trieste, the bookshops on Fillmore, Union Street's galleries where an original Mucha or Benny Bufano might hang on the wall, dance, music—it's a town where international talents want to swing. And if sports is your game, this is where Willie Mays, one of baseball's immortal heroes hammered long balls for the hometown Giants. Then for years, Joe Montana, golden boy quarterback of the mighty 49ers football squad, revolutionized the game with aerial blitzkriegs that became identified as the West Coast offence.

As any bartender could tell you, "What's not to like about a city of winners?"

Despite the hills and cable cars, it remains a city for walking and roaming. Year by year though, you'd see the architecture growing tonier as rents and house prices soared. Painted Lady gingerbread homes began emerging as spectacular ornamented showpiece inns; gay culture vibrated from Castro Street; crackheads in the Mission District got moved elsewhere, and even that once dead-end part of town would find itself with a glitzy new art museum. The Marina District's flatlands started coming alive with clubs where acts like Van Morrison's daughter Shana held down the bandstand. You looked up from your breakfast in the morning and saw signed photos on the wall from Tony Bennett and artists who liked eating in the same place as you.

When you meet a few people, a town takes on a life of its own. Mike Bloomfield, the brilliant blues guitarist whose *East-West* sounds in 1966 helped pave the way for a generation seeking insight, told me one night after a gig in Arcata that he'd been playing in a club in San Francisco. That got me to the Coffee Galley on Grant Avenue not far from City Lights. A bohemian joint since the fifties when Beats like Bob Kaufman and Ferlinghetti read there, it helped introduce Janis Joplin, who sang as a young Texas folkie when she first hit town. Down from Humboldt County, I night-owled around North Beach looking for love, checking the Basque restaurant off Broadway, and digging the sounds—Nick Gravenites maybe, or Jimmy Reed in one of his last shows at the Savoy.

This is a city of neighbourhoods. Jim Koller, a careful poet, publisher of *Coyote's Journal*, and one of the original Haight-Ashbury Diggers, was filling me in why we had to see and experience the Coit Tower on Telegraph Hill. "You'll see the allegorical murals from the proletarian 1930s," he said as we walked through the Lower Haight. "Marvellous work, uplifting. They show you the soul of this place—the dignity of labour. California as an agricultural division of paradise." We caught a bus up Van Ness past the old Avalon Ballroom, and Jim nodded at the site in his usual matter-of-fact style; he'd been friends with the Grateful Dead who helped keep the psychedelic scene grooving in the sixties.

From Russian Hill it's a pleasant walk through gleaming white residential streets to the tower. The view of San Francisco Bay and the breeze is spectacular: this is where Sir Francis Drake cruised by, on the run after his sack of the Spanish-Pacific coast from Valparaiso to Lima in 1579. The well-known parrots here that have escaped or been returned to the wild lend a crazy, colourful zing to the hilltop and surrounding streets; surely the steep crowded slopes jammed with multi-level homes with small eclectic gardens are among the world's funkiest districts.

Jim started out in North Beach and knew the hill inside out. "The tower has twenty-five murals from the Depression years. It's the city's best gallery," he reckoned as we took it in. The style, after Mexican pioneers like Diego Rivera, is heroic. These are humble workers, you feel their toil and hardships, and in more crowded works that reflect city life, you sense the joy, the busyness, the machinery and bustle of a world on the move. It's impossible not to see the loyalty and humility of these California workers—working-class immigrants, farmers, and tradespeople, as well as their contemporary business counterparts, all within the framing eyes of a lush growing landscape, or a surging city dynamic. You cannot turn away unmoved from their dignified Social Realist depictions of daily life in California's agricultural valleys. Standing before them, you feel proud to be a human being, in solidarity with these men and women, the salt of the Earth. Jim Koller made you feel this way too.

Francis Drake, experts finally agreed, landed and repaired his boats at Point Reyes, north of the city. It's an ecological jewel, one of the Pacific Flyway's most beloved birding sites. Since the time of Scottish-American John Muir, who founded and served as first president of the Sierra Club, California and San Francisco have been forward in wilderness protection and conservationist thinking. The hamlet of Bolinas, an hour's drive from the city, survives as an insular community with an outsized literary importance that has been remarkable. Richard Brautigan, the wacky, surrealist poet-novelist of *Trout Fishing in America* fame and Jim Koller's best pal, lived and died here. For a settlement of not much larger than fifteen hundred souls, it has been home to a glistening roster of writers and artists; poets Joanne Kyger, Philip Whalen, Robert Creeley; and musicians Rambling Jack Elliot, Jim Carroll, Grace Slick, and Paul Kantner among them.

On a walk one morning with Kyger down the lane from her little house to the village paper that she edited for decades, she mentioned her approach to writing books. "You pay attention to the moment, to the detail," she said, her short greying hair like a badge of wisdom. "Maybe it's more a part of meditative open consciousness like what Ginsberg was talking about—language and the architecture of liberation—but the body is a vehicle for consciousness too."

Around Bolinas Bay, above Muir Beach, the friendly rival hamlet of Stinson Beach is the micro-pod where Ken Kesey and the Grateful Dead worked out the fine-tuning on the Acid Tests; where they'd get the San Francisco countercultural project of the sixties off the launchpad. What a nexus! And off the sky-road above, is the Zen Center's cozy, disciplined Green Gulch Farm and Buddhist practice centre. These many streams flow into and help make the city sparkle. In San Francisco you are never far from the water.

The coastline here is eternally vibrant. Standing beside the Great Pacific Highway not far from Golden Gate Park, one hears the sea crash on the rocks and scents the salt tang and cypress groves in the spray. Something important is going on, another thread in the warp and weft of life. For more than a century, San Francisco has been one of the world's true Renaissance cities, serving as a critical incubator of alternative ideas regarding the whole notion of personal liberation—a city of refuge, befitting its very name in honour of the blessed peacemaker, Saint Francis of Assisi.

It has become expensive too. Silicon Valley, its wealth and sudden millionaires continue making headlines, yet it's difficult not to see how the Asian insight traditions of meditation and yoga or the human potential and modern ecological awakenings we take for granted now are intrinsically linked with this place.

In his oracular essay, "Buddhism and the Coming Revolution" from *Earth House Hold,* poet Gary Snyder crystallizes the fundamental importance of these awakenings: "The mercy of the West has been social revolution; the mercy of the East has been individual insight into the basic self/void. We need both."

You can't argue with that.

I think of San Francisco, its hilly streets, the wild parrots, and the food and drink here that recalls Europe but remains quintessentially American. I think of its poetry and music, the beauty of its white Mediterranean houses, and the Asian culture that diffuses through here into the West. The Hispanic world covers its streets. Tony Bennett, a New Yorker, who gave the town its signature tune, reckoned wistfully that he left his heart here. Each time I return, it's another chance to recapture a piece of my own.

1968-2017

DOWN LIGHTHOUSE LANE

We rattled out of Negril down Lighthouse Lane honking and waving goodbye. The blue-green Caribbean spangled and shimmered on our left as the waves rolled in, breaking on the stony shoulders of the little bay where Delbert lived near Palm Grove. Goodbye tar-paper shanties in parched, hilly bush land; goodbye fishnet menders on the beach. All the folks we'd met along the coast were left behind as our reckless driver sped us off on bald tires toward the twilight.

Goodbye island fields and guesthouse yards littered with coco husk; goodbye flour sack clothing billowing on wash lines, and the scraps of fading posters and slogans—Two Is Better Than Too Many! Red Stripe Beer!—that flaked off the baked mud walls. Goodbye to the fruit sellers and the pudding man up Terrace Walk. Goodbye Jamaica, clatters of people idling about your dusty roadsides.

Then a last glance and a wave at the plaza with its moneychangers, flashy Honda scooter boys, takeaway shack promising "Food, No Frills," and hustlers and hawkers flogging every conceivable local commodity.

"Change sum dollars today, mon?"

"Sum'tin for your head today, bruddah?"

"Sinsemilla, cocaine…got de ganga, mon; de verrah best bud, mon…"

Down at the beach where the river empties from out of the mountains, the Rastamen sit in a shady grove sucking on sugar sticks, watching the world rock by. Women clad in colours as wild as tropical birdlife shuckle past in twos and threes, baskets of mango and oranges atop their heads. At the Ital-Vital health shop and the shack, the heavy throb and croon of island dub sounds—Yellowman, the Mighty Diamonds, Toots Hibbert—drifts out to the bay. A shine-head boy no more than seven or eight stops in the road at the sounds and starts breaking down, working through his best stepping moves, snapping his fingers, dipping his knees, spinning barefoot in the dust, then walks on by, nodding "*Irie*, mon!"

Cooking fires charge the air with an unmistakable charcoal fragrance: chicken and green bananas, conch in pepper soup, curried goat. Hot jerked pork sizzles in a hubcap grill.

On the rocks near our paddy hut, the Rastaman from up the hill trail throws out his line every day, marking time with hard tugs and chants to call up the fish the way his father used to do. Hunkered down with tough black feet on the jagged lava rock, he slings line and sinker around his head like David before the giant, jet skin gleaming in fierce mid-day heat. With the tight body of an NFL linebacker, he chants methodically: "Rasta, Rasta, Rasta… Com dem fish. Rasta, Rasta. He say He will provide. Come fish, come."

It's a simple life. I ask him if all is well. "Yes, mon" he says. "We have every'ting we need in this world, yes. De Lord give us every'ting. He gave us de skillness and wiseness to catch fish. Yes, mon. We don't want for nut'ing. Is paradise, mon. Jamaica is de most beautiful country. Yes."

Last week, Delbert our strolling partner, slapped his own younger brother for trying to cheat us over the price of a hand line and some tackle in the market; told us, "Ev'ryone take advantage you here, mon. I can give you dis same line for nutin'. People must live together in 'armony. We can't have dis war trouble. Is tribal. Is Babylon, mon."

Delbert, with razor weal down his cheek, sounds like Bob Marley, all the discs we've loved through the years—"Don't Rock the Boat," "Trench Town Rock," "Natural Mystic," that bubbling steady reggae rhythm. I've wanted to go out with him, fishing before sunrise when he paddles his dugout coco-trunk canoe out to the horizon, but he knows danger better than I do. Back by mid-morning after baiting up the bay with conch for the next day's working, he hauls his baskets of catch—yellowtail, conch, lobster, needlefish—to the market truck headed for Sav La Mar down the island. Delbert, with a body as taut and lean as a billfish, whose sweetheart never leaves the shadows of their hut. Who asked us to stay and move into the mountains with him and grow ganja where no troopers could ever find us. Delbert, catching soldier crabs for my bait-hooks. Goodbye, Goodbye.

We go away to leave behind the everydayness, to find paradise around a bend and live, at least for a time, in sweet nepenthe. The exquisite beauty of the flowers and shrubs, the chickens and rooting pigs about the door keep us calm and a little crazy. Is this what Gauguin saw when he ran off to Tahiti, already sick, to paint his vision of a purer creation? The sunshine, the water clearer than dreams, the Blue Mountains where the coffee comes from tell us who we are; and when the dream is done, we understand exactly where we belong after all. Goodbye, Goodbye.

"You like dese lobstah? Maybe you like cooking 'em tonight for a good price?" The pudding man comes around every two days, sometimes with fish and sweet blood oranges. A grandfather and still fit, tight all over, with a thin white jaw-line beard: "Maybe today you like some mushroom from de forest?"

In a photograph a Frenchman sent us later—he'd been living in a shack nearby—I am standing in the doorway to our cabin in a loose shirt, baggy cotton trousers and holding a walking stick I'd been carving. My beard is grown in; my longish hair pulled back in the Celtic style, salted down with seawater. We'd been picking wild fruit up the hillside. Life was simple, and we were eating well; Kwan-shik was a young beauty, and I was writing and fishing every day. There wasn't much else than the reading, but books were scarce unless you bummed a lift up to Mo'Bay. Montego was where the Queen would slip in on the royal yacht Britannia for a wave to the crowds while we were in the area. Bands in the street, parades, bunting, they loved her in JA. Everyone dressed like for a holiday.

I look at the doorway photo now and see that it was living in Negril that really gave me an understanding of Gauguin the painter. When he ran off to Tahiti, he changed the way modern art looks at the world. Before that, he recuperated on the French island of Martinique in 1887.

His Caribbean paintings depict the lushness of the tropics and serve as the training run for his epic shot at glory in the South Seas.

The island's small-scale service economy works for both sides. The country people check you out during these transactions, calling up to your door. Little by little, you are brought further into the community. You wave hello walking up and down the lane. A young fellow on a push-bike with a carrier of eggs, all sizes, different colours, asks if you're coming to the dance on Saturday night. "Where's that?"

"Jus'up de road."

The expensive all-inclusive resorts are up the road too, but in the other direction where everybody has their hand out all the time. Tourists fly in for a package deal in the sun; to drink rum shooters and bonk their brains out in the tropics. Walled hotels with dreamy names build swimming pools adjacent to the ocean for suntanning without the hassle of getting sand in your shorts. You can count on seeing someone walk by in a t-shirt proclaiming "Sex is the most fun you have without laughing in JA!" German blondes chase giddily after local studs, and schoolgirls will patiently braid their silky hair in cornrows down on the beach. Among the expertly manicured grounds and bird-of-paradise blooms, there are signs warning Beware of Falling Coconuts.

It's not all a reality television set: hotel workers converse in the gardens, and their singsong patois and flirting laughter carries through. Occasional honks burst in from passing trucks in the distance. You'll spot a heap of fresh coconuts beside an outdoor bar, future rum cocos for the poolside trade, and it's hard to resist the thirst that can come upon you seeing them. Behind it all, the eternal blue wash of rollers breaking ashore from the west as other travellers arrive and trickle through to the outdoor cafés—young Norwegians, Finns, an older Swiss couple, one or two whispering Anglos. Look about though, and there'll be a spot where they've vanished. Beachfront décor here is imaginative: polished hardwoods, varnished coco-palm beams as solid as concrete, cabanas made of interlaced rattan, cool floor tiles underfoot. For that painterly moment, search for a quiet nook near a back wall in soft yellow emulsion, shady with mauve or magenta hibiscus, and a Victorian white-spindle railing all around.

Outside the resorts near the pop-up bars and charcoal cook shacks for the tourists, you'll find a dropout or two hustling a smidge of work. "Him Bob singing again," Delbert nodded to a lean dreadlocked mainlander from the U.S. or Canada. "Him had a tax problem," Del continued, and I got the story. Rather than declare bankruptcy and try to work himself out of debt for the next five to twenty-five years, Bob decided to just leave and see if anybody noticed. You'd see him busking mornings against a shade tree in his wool toque, strumming his three or four rhythms on guitar for the newcomers—popular tunes by Neil Young, Bob Marley, the Eagles, the Beatles. He had a couple of island tunes, a Christmas song he'd sing over and over, "When Irish Eyes Are Smiling" for St Paddy's Day, and "Hava Nagila" for the New Yorkers. Delbert shrugged as we walked by: "He still living 'ere somewhere in a skanky cabin with him local wife who flips his rotis. Babylon children. No prabhlem…"

It gets quieter when you leave the centre of the small town and look for less commercial guesthouses toward the Lighthouse. You can find a long-stay cabin with a sea breeze and a propane cooker. The beaches are still; there's no daily riot going on. Standing in the water, you can gaze up at the hillside and listen in the heat as a slow, heavy dub thumps out to the bay from someone's open door.

Jamaican economics is based on one proposition: Buy for a little less than it's worth, sell for as much above that as you can get. Miss Bea, our landlady, worked the margins with consummate skill on every transaction: never gouging, but never quite doing anyone a favour, no exceptions; business was always business, yet never harsh; her thumb figured discreetly upon almost every deal along her stretch of the lane.

Delbert, our friend, made exceptions. He lived as lean and hard a life as anyone we've known, yet seemed to lack for little. Six days a week he rowed out in the dark, beyond sight in his dugout, working the sea. Never had I seen a more physically attuned specimen: pure bone and muscle, sinews tight from constant exertion, not a trace of fat. Watching the sun go down, we'd enjoy a bottle of Red Stripe beer against a small canteen wall along a piece of road where every half-mile has its own holiness church and preacher. "Positive vibrations, bruddah," he'd incant affably with his quiet smile. He didn't know yet about the "shugah," what they call diabetes in patois. The next time we'd come to see him, he'd be gone.

I thought I saw him one time later though. Wandering in a druid state of mind past the Green Turtle Inn, along a narrow neck of road stretched between the Caribbean and a green marsh up West End Road where the boys dive from the cliffs, we came across an ibis in the empty courtyard of an old island politician. Tawny rather than snowy, with a beautifully curved bill, it turned on its thin nimble legs and stared at us. I heard it whisper, "Stick to what you do, bruddah. Get ready for dat higher place will come." It was a very hot day with the sun directly overhead, and I should have worn a hat. You could see the heat rising in waves. The ibis looked at us again then pecked downward with its red-orange bill. We'd be leaving again soon. Goodbye Jamaica. Goodbye, Goodbye Negril.

It has grown busier here along the coast, and there are more permanent signs for American corporations with the jobs they bring. I don't think Delbert would have worn a brown or khaki uniform for one of them. The spartan country churches and preachers are still here; and so are a growing number of returnees who have moved back to the island from London or Birmingham, comfortable with their pensions after working long years in England's hospitals and factories.

A walk along Jamaica's country roads is part exercise in self-preservation and part sheer sensual sensation, like being inside a box of painter's colours. Vehicles tear about at speed, nuts and bolts shaking and rattling, ripping around corners in the bush. Bicycles and horse-drawn carts go by. People still give you a wave, though not quite as often for the resorts are moving further along the coast and buying up land. Whether it is a successful holiday destination or not rests with the traveller and what you are seeking. The colours and island gaiety remain astonishing, and the edginess and grist of human experience on display within its exquisite tropical land and seascapes keeps it a challenge. You must stick with it, as Delbert and the ibis insist from the higher heights, surely a metaphor for some deeper human need, the kind Bob Marley sang about, on which faith and authenticity are built.

1981-2014

LISBON'S IBERIAN SOUL

PORTUGAL

B.B. King told me once during an interview that he loved playing in Lisbon because "people there really understand the blues." He ought to know.

I hadn't been to the old Iberian port city, but I knew the Romans had been there, following Hannibal and the Carthaginians. What the original Celtic tribes had to say about all that has been forgotten, but we can imagine. Anyway, the Celts know how to endure, and the blues still run deep here. Reinventing themselves as the Portuguese, they made a comeback under the aegis of Prince Henry the Navigator and ushered in Europe's Age of Discovery in the 15th century, thereby providing politically correct academics with the reliably safe topic of "decolonization" to thrash over during the current juncture. In more modern times, the dictator Dr. António de Oliveira Salazar found his way into power here. Few absolute leaders have lived a more austere life than the highly religious, fascist bachelor, Dr. Salazar. For forty years he ruled from the presidential palace in Lisbon's Belém district, while Portugal remained one of Europe's poorest countries.

Lisbon is "the Little Paris"—an exquisitely beautiful old town with friendly people, sea air, terrific meals everywhere, great wine, and soulful fado singers. One of Europe's most appealing cities, its architecture is picturesque, and transportation by trams or taxi is funky, inexpensive, and simple to negotiate. No other town has a sweeter tooth, and the number of coffee houses and *pastelerias,* or pastry shops, for passing the morning and watching the world go by is unrivalled. The national passion for *natas,* the small, thick custard tarts, runs deep here, and the bakery where they originated is three or four doors from one of the steadiest pensions in Belém, the place where we like to stay. Crowds line up from early morning to taste them, but you can buy these scrumptious goodies on practically any corner. If you're a sports nut, Portugal understands that too: Lisbon has a pair of world-class *futbol* teams to root for, working-class Benfica and Sporting: Belém is the perennial three's-a-crowd underdog; Porto, from the country's north coast, is a powerhouse challenger.

An Irish friend, who knows Lisbon inside out, gave us gilt-edged instructions for walking about. "If you're a writer, you're going to love it," she told us. "And don't miss the sunset hour for a drink—have a good glass of something with authority, fergodzakes." And she winked: 'It's only a sin if you take pleasure in it..."

She must have been talking to my father.

Belém district on the Tagus River near the celebrated Monasterio de Jeronimo where the Portuguese mariners set sail for their history-changing voyages in the 15th century is a good bet for a decent sleep in affordable lodgings. You're also smack on the wide riverfront, so enjoy the view. It's an easy rumbling ride to downtown on the pre-World War I #15 tram which is a delight in itself—a single self-propelled carriage that looks like a cable car from San Francisco, and they leave the wooden windows open to catch the breeze. There's a tranquil park for morning exercise and meditation or reading, and enough walking destinations to keep you from meltdown in Lisbon's busier tourist areas. The culprits here are the enormous saltwater cruise liners that tie up within close walking distance of everything, disgorging thousands of passengers. Consider the impact of two of these docking at one time: It's a phenomenon affecting tourist destination cities and even former remote islands around the world.

Lisbon is a pretty town built on hills—seven of them—and it's delicious to the eye. Hillsides are crammed with their own distinct neighbourhoods, and dwellings and their red-tiled roofs beat with a southern European pulse. Earthquakes aren't kind to brick and plaster exteriors, and the city suffered a devastating quake in 1755. Its rebuilding essentially shaped the historic centre with ornate features, gables, portals, and the beguiling opera windows that you see while walking about.

The historic city is not built high, but the traceries and embellishments that skilled masons can add to a building give it character. Simply walking about Lisbon's historic, narrow, shady streets and little lanes is unforgettable; an especially lovely sight is the *azulejos:* glazed painted tiles set in the walls and entranceways of homes and public facades. Normally a deep blue, similar to Delft, azulejos light up a façade. We first saw these in Asia's old-time Portuguese settlements—Malacca in Malaysia has a couple of streets that survive with a feeling of bygone days, and the Goa coast along the Arabian Sea in western India has plenty. There's timelessness in painted tiles. Technically speaking, they serve multiple purposes, and there's a reason why you see them in hot countries. Easy to keep clean, they are durable and help maintain coolness of temperature.

Portugal has had a long run as a Catholic nation. As you'd imagine, Lisbon's cathedrals are spectacular; however, the dramatic Igreja Santa Maria in Belém that's contiguous with the Monasterio de Jeronimo also serves as the resting place for two of Portugal's greatest heroes. The seadog navigator Vasco de Gama, who cracked the Arab monopoly on Asia's spice trade with Europe in 1488, rests in a huge memorial tomb adjacent to the tomb of Portugal's greatest poet, Luís de Camões (1527–1580), author of *The Lusiads,* a series of cantos that chronicle the history-changing voyages of Portugal's mariners and their European rediscovery of India. This Renaissance showpiece was completed in 1601 after a century of construction funded with a tax on Portugal's voluptuously profitable spice trade in pepper, cinnamon, cloves, and cardamom out of Africa and the Far East.

The Portuguese understand that food is not a commodity to be primped and cooed over; it's a pleasure that's also a necessity, a gift to be savoured daily. As in France and among other civilized peoples, you find restaurant menus posted near the door. It's a treat to enjoy the coolness of an evening walkabout and browse assorted menus. Find your haunt and settle in with a dish of olives, a basket of crunchy bread, and a glass or three of wine. The first two are Mediterranean staples; the cost is negligible, and only calorie counters decline them. Seafood and pork are the stable foundations of a cuisine here that's wholesome, hearty and just plain downhome *yummy*. Grilled fresh sardines, grouper and parrotfish, *bacalhao* or salt cod, shellfish, pork in stew, duck—it's all here. As you'd expect, Portugal knows about wine with decent Douro reds, but the star of the show is the chilled green wine, the *vinho verde*, a young wine with a little effervescence, preferred in warmer weather. Like a proper meal in Greece or France, a dinner in Lisbon is an identifying badge of the city and her people. These folks know how to live—even a small farmhouse cheese is a pleasure with a walloping large glass of ruby or dry Port, from well, *Port*ugal, and a bill that won't give you indigestion.

With Portugal's long colonial legacy, Lisbon has its share of Goan Indian, Macao-style Cantonese, and Brazilian eating places. It makes for a fabulous eating mosaic. Portugal is not as cheap as, say, Mexico, but it's one of the best deals in Europe. With a friendly, fairly egalitarian society, Lisbon benefits from all of this without the self-conscious, official multiculturalism of places like Canada or Australia. Almost everyone speaks some English now, making it easy to get about and meet people.

We were dropping our key off at the front desk of our pension one evening, when the smart young Goanese clerk asked, "You like to hear some music tonight?"

"You bet. Any idea where we go to hear the fado?"

"Ah, then you go to Alfama. It comes from that place..."

We gestured thanks with a wave and moved on into the night. Alfama, the old Moorish quarter, is a stiff five-or ten-minute walk uphill from the Santa Apolonia metro station beside the river. You recognize it as a neighbourhood of narrow cobbled streets that intersect the principal walking lane of Rua Remedios. Fado is synonymous with *saudade,* a sense of longing, or yearning—with the blues in Portuguese. The Welsh, another Celtic people from a small coastal country of hills and valleys, call it their *heireth.* In Lisbon it's a birthright associated with the traditional waterfront poor, and they use it to bring on down the *soul.* Neither as showy nor dramatic as the flamenco next door in southern Spain, it's deeper, and more profound, almost a religious expression. Women in black shawls *yearn* here, they don't wail. Chesty male tenors resonate over the *guitarras,* and suddenly we're in the deep end of nostalgia and love, with emotive lyrics and melodic figures plucked on the nationalistically unique Portuguese *guitarra*, round and slender, with its inescapable North African heritage.

The Arcaz Velho at Calçada do Forte is an atmospheric local joint, nothing fancy but welcoming in the old way, less commercial than the upscale saloons a couple of streets away that cater to the cruise ship crowd. Never mind 'em. The young woman who runs the place, Daniela Giblott, is the MC and sings. There are thirty or forty seats in the house. Her mother, Elvira, is a veteran *fadista,* and the pair of them will leave you wrung out, especially mom, who's got Edith Piaf's salt in her veins. Or you might catch them joined by a trad male singer like João Soeiro, and a brace of the most intense guitarists in the city. Batten down the hatches, make ready for a night of it.

Unless you're in the sticks somewhere up the coast, where it's likely more of a local drop-in session, a night of fado is an all-evening affair. For a set price, you get you a long, lazy dinner with green fisherman's soup of cabbage and seaweed, salad, a main plate—*bacalhau* à *Bras,* or codfish fried rice, that's effectively a national dish; tasty octopus, or pork medallions in sauce—and plates of olives, bread, and a regional cheese to get you going. Snooty wine lists? Don't worry; they fix you up with a jug of chilled *vinho verde*, then coffee and dessert later on. The music and entertainment is included: Figure on thirty to forty euros for the whole affair; live large, fellow slave! It's worth every penny. Life is short. You can spend double that nearby, but why bother? You haven't lived until the fado women start lamenting their *saudade*. Trust B.B. King—they know about the blues here; it gets mystical, the way that Son House or Rev. Gary Davis transport themselves beyond sorrow in their southern Delta blues, using blues to transcend the blues. Can we get an *Amen?*

We were in a romantic haze—the vinho verde helps—between sets when the singers and guitarists take a breather. "This has to be where Dennis Pavao got it from, that's for sure," Kwan-shik whispered. Honolulu's beloved pop vocalist, Dennis Pavao—a beautiful guy with flowers in his hair—brought life back to Hawaii's high-pitched falsetto vocal style during the 1970s. A hundred years ago, when Portuguese labourers emigrated out to the islands to cut sugarcane, they brought their compact guitars and mandolins with them, ultimately giving the world their most famous gift, the *ukulele,* and a way of singing that became identifiably Hawaiian. Unless Tiny Tim walks through the door, you're not likely to hear falsetto in Alfama, but the style and projection of the male singers especially is uncannily familiar if you know and love Hawaiian-style vocals.

You'll exit at one or two in the morning, suitably wobbly, but there are plenty of people still roaming the quiet streets in Lisbon; it feels secure here, no menace. Any bad actors are usually bumming around the Rossio district, a respectable distance off uptown. Ramble on, keeping your wits about you, as ever. The trams run late and are cheap as chips. Taxis are as affordable as they get in Europe.

Trams are the colourful way to traverse Lisbon's often-steep hills. The fabled #28 winds about the old city on its forty-to-forty-five-minute run, chugging up and down through four or five distinct neighbourhoods, including steep downhill runs, remarkably tight bends; a hop-on/hop-off, tank-engined little terrier of a tram. Bumble-bee yellow and looking like something out of a carnival rides museum, the #28 is the most fun in town. Roll down the window, get out your notebook, and be ready: You'll be trucking past kitchen windows, draper's shop counters, and corner markets. Palaces, statues, chi-chi lounges, you get it all.

"Don't miss Sintra" the tourists say. Tucked away up in the hills, Sintra is a popular day trip out of Lisbon. Like the Simla hills in India, the altitude keeps it cooler in the hot season, and Lisbon is no stranger to 40°C summertime temperatures. Wordsworth's politically minded poet chum Robert Southey believed this was the loveliest spot in the world, and one supposes Sintra is a decent place to wuggle about. The downside is that it takes some trouble to get there, chugging an hour each way by train through Lisbon's working-class Benfica suburbs, tattered with graffiti and housing long blocks of slummy flats, yet also the home of one of Europe's great football teams. Not our cup of tea though. After a quick look about, we grabbed a coffee and *nata* then jumped a bus and zigzagged down through the mountains to Cascais back on the coast. This ride is a hoot. You might be in bandit country with rascally country characters and fabulous scenery all the way.

Cascais is a shapely seaside community forty-five minutes from Lisbon by train, and a two-kilometre walk from the casino resort, Estoril. Originally a fishing village, its Lisbon Riviera location has attracted modern apartments and moderate-sized hotels. The waterfront plazas are full of seafood restaurants and bars, with Brazilian jazz combos playing in the streets. There are beaches for a dip and a fishing pier for watching kids jumping off. It's a low-rise town that feels and looks upscale—a kind of Portuguese southern California—but the tourism impact isn't overwhelming, and prices remain affordable. It's a fun place to knock about. We copped the train back with a shared coffee and loaf of cornbread to munch between us.

On our return journey, we met a Frenchwoman from Lyons. "I am researching the pilgrimage route from Lisbon, through Portugal to Santiago de Compostella," she informed us, glad of some company during her solo venture. We were immediately interested. "The *pellerins*, the pilgrims, mostly follow the Spanish route to the cathedral at Compostella," our new friend explained, "but the route *Portugais* is a little shorter, about 600 kilometres, and it's quieter in the Portugal countryside; not so many walkers."

The pilgrimage route through northern Spain to the holy shrine of St. James in Compostella on the Atlantic is a rugged 800-kilometre trek from the Spanish-French border across the Basque hill country of northern Spain. Since the 1960s, it has manifested itself anew for a troubled generation as a personal, spiritual quest route along the ancient pilgrims' trail. Until meeting our French companion, we hadn't heard of a Portuguese route; it has definite appeal. As Marie-France detailed, from Lisbon you get clear of the city bustle, walk northward toward Porto, and thence into Spain. It's an alternative that still leaves abundant time for a Chaucer-flavoured journey, meeting fellow wanderers on the road to the shrine.

Portugal may be a small nation; however, its history is sprawling. Her mariners freebooted around Africa and out to Asia before anyone else in Europe. They colonized widely, getting into China and out in the Indonesian archipelago as far as Timor. The prize was spices—light, portable, and an unbelievably high-value cargo. Simultaneously, in Macao, the Jesuits would settle themselves in preparation for a long campaign of saving souls in China.

The colonial legacy still vibrates: In Africa, five nations still speak Portuguese, as does the South American colossus, Brazil. The result is a unique cultural mélange. Lisbon has its share of impressive art museums, and Portuguese literature punches above its weight. Beginning with Camões, its heavy-hitting writers include Fernando Pessoa, a poet and essayist of the early 20th century; the 19th century social-reformer novelist José Maria de Eca de Queirós; and the quirky Nobel Prize 1998 laureate, Jose Saramango.

At Lisbon you are not far from Fatima, one of the Catholic world's most revered shrines. As these things go, Kwan-shik and I had both lost our mothers within a few days of each other some months before, and although unsure of what we might expect, we made our way to Sete Rios, the central bus station, one morning and booked coach tickets for a day's pilgrimage. You do not set off expecting to be shaken; of course, as a pilgrim you expect *something*, but what exactly is hard to say.

Just around the corner from the station, we passed a Jewish restaurant with a Star of David displayed in a window. It's the job of pilgrims to notice what they notice: "An ecumenical commencement," I murmured.

We found the pilgrim bus, a modern comfortable coach; couples old and young were boarding, groups of travellers and families. There were national flags on backpacks—Poles, Kiwis, a Czech, Africans in national dress. Children were well-behaved. In a seat in front of us, an Afro-Brazilian woman with elaborately braided hair blessed herself and some teenage girls before the ride. Then we set off, like a summer mystery trip when we were children, exciting.

Lisbon's suburbs stretch for a long way; blocks of apartments for the young, housing for urban workers. This was not Benfica. We passed attractively designed buildings and small bungalows, and six-to eight-unit townhomes, all with sloping roofs for the catchwater. There were smart districts with long views of the water and tidy landscaping that give way to dry low hills and olive groves on the hillsides.

Outside the windows, fields and hedges, small farm holdings, tile-roofed houses. Canola in bloom; small, compact towns along the way. White walls, umber tiles; tight, tidy demarcated property lines. Sheep near grapevines, then vines set among cypress and low stands of evergreen, all reminiscent of Horace in his *Satires* and *Epodes* from Augustan Rome, writing on the land, offering his moving prayers in praise of life in the countryside. Hadn't the Romans ventured out here to the edge of the Atlantic, to Iberia?

Fatima lies in hilly land; along the way, modern windmills generate electricity on the higher ridges, and stone quarries have been cut into either side of the road. A long stepped field has been measured off, milled into heavy stone blocks, heaven knows how long ago. The land here is raw stone, a thin inch or two of crushed lava-like dirt litters the stony fields atop. The bus ride to Fatima itself shrinks time.

Arriving at a small spotless station, we begin our trek. Directional signs point the way for pilgrims. Ten minutes up the road, we come upon a vast white square with statues here and there. A huge white modern edifice nearly as large as a covered stadium sits immovably before us, and a historical-looking church perches on a rise at the far end of the plaza. Throughout the huge plaza, pilgrims worship at small chapels or sanctuaries in bright sunshine. More to check it off some imaginary list, we enter the white complex where a beggar waits at the door.

It reveals itself as a gigantic super-modern church, devotionally named for the Holy Trinity. We size up the calm enormous interior, then proceed down the low raked centre aisle. A massive subtle altar mural made of spangled, gold-leaf terracotta plates presents an iconic, mystical image of the Holy Mother surrounded by children and disciples. But it is the sculpture of Nossa Senhora de Fátima nearby that is extraordinary. In the blue-white image created from a ten-foot block of Carrara marble by the Italian artist Benedetto Pietrogrande, she is young, simple, her left foot stepping forward a little, and in the light that is filtered effectively from above, the image appears to hover like an apparition. Notably, her hands are not in prayer like Our Lady in other places. Her left hand points down to the ground, the *mudra* of touching the Earth; the right hand is raised in the *mudra* of gracious welcome. Her eyes gaze forward, cast down a little, the entire presence motherly, divine, ethereal. To stand in the presence of this image is overpowering, spiritual, and leaves men and women weeping.

Awed, I whispered, "This is the traditional mudra of the Buddha and of Kuan-Yin, the Goddess of Mercy all through Asia." As quintessentially as Michelangelo, the artist captured an interfaith spirit, full of grace, but more subtle, different. Here you bring your imagination. It's beautiful to see that the church can be so progressive. Modern and still classical. Within the unstained field of altar gold everyone is blessed, all are holy. The crucifix is simple, modern. Overcome with emotion for our mothers, we left cleansed with a sense of grace.

Outside, at the Chapel of the Apparitions and other sites, pilgrims were on their knees, praying, hoping for miracles, lighting candles, doing all the things they had come so far to do in expressing their reverence. A procession of African pilgrims sang, led by their priests and community elders. I offered a prayer for their safe travels.

Beyond the sanctuary area, we approached the shops and memento sellers that are part of every shrine, it seems. At a coffee garden, we stopped for a cold drink while a group of Asian visitors bustled past, worried they were late for something, their guide urging them forward. Two older women grumbled at having to rush; I couldn't blame them. We were back in the ordinary world again.

2018

A DESERT MANTRA

I was staying with friends on the edge of the New Mexico desert north of Santa Fe. Living space is tight and expensive in town, so my friends make their home in a metal Quonset hut fronting an arroyo, a dry drainage canyon that is home to many beautiful birds. My first morning, the opportunity to simply sit outside and be still was perfect. Nothing focuses you on new territory quite like finding a clear spot, remaining quiet, and taking in the sounds, hums, buzzes, glints of light, and things that move around you.

The high desert can be off-putting at first contact; it's a hard place, arid and windblown, the landscape dominated by the sky, the air clear and thin. With altitude from six to eight thousand feet, the first few days breathing is a little laboured. The vistas of weathered mesas and bluffs are extraordinary, primordial, and unlike anything else on the planet. You half expect to see dinosaurs walk out of them. Definitive Cowboy and Indian country: desert vegetation tough and thorny; knee-high buckskin leggings or cowboy boots make sense. I hit the late spring bloom right on time: prickly carpets of cactus flowers alive with birdlife. Not even the jungles of Southeast Asia or Hawaii present such a din. It's intoxicating, a desert mantra.

Santa Fe itself is hard to get hold of. Half historic architectural exposition, half adobe theme park, the community of 83,000 feels like a fifth of that. The visitor industry is central to the town's lifeblood, and local residents maintain a well-defined Southwestern ambience: no large or loud commercial signage, no florescent backlighting, comparatively little commercial detritus. It can be hard to find places as a result, since even the streets are marked only demurely for passersby.

Santa Fe has more than one hundred commercial art galleries—a major component of its economy and the third-highest concentration of private galleries in the country after New York and Los Angeles. Artists have long ventured to this area: D.H. Lawrence lived two hours north in Taos, his final resting place marked by a remote and beautiful shrine—kept up in simple and unaffected condition. The poets Auden and Robinson Jeffers came here and worked, as did painter Georgia O'Keefe, who spent most of her time interpreting the desert landscape around Abiqui.

The native traditions, all still active, are Pueblo, Navajo, Mescalero Apache, and Hopi. The large prominent Navajo communities make prized and costly art and handcrafts. Friends introduced me to a pair of Navajo women artists, and once we'd gotten past the initial reserve, they were especially welcoming. I cooked for them my last night in town, and Gabriela, a printmaking instructor at the Institute of Indian Art, talked about the story of Blue Corn Boy and White Pollen Girl, and how each is also alter ego of the other. As she unwound her tale, it sounded every bit as mythic and lovely as the East Asian story of the cowherd girl and her sweetheart in the stars.

Gabriela went on to invite my friends and me to her family home at Four Corners reserve near the majestic Canyon de Chelly. The Navajo have strong healing traditions, and their desert medicine includes Star Gazing, crystal and rock healing, Dream medicine and a fascinating elder known as the Hand Trembler.

Old family arguments exist among the desert First Nations peoples, but the local wisdom is that the various groups split off from an original family. The Navajo, my friends said, feel some guilt about having raided the more sedentary Pueblo people who lived in the well-known and unique adobe tenement-style complexes. Before all these tribal offshoots though, the Anasazi aboriginal culture settled the region.

The Anasazi vanished, but their civilization remains long after them. These were the cliff dwellers, people who dug out homes from the sandstone bluffs, cutting terraces to walk upon, using ladders to visit up and down to each other's homes, and sharing agricultural labour in communal corn patches along arroyo water channels. The evidence they have left is of a well-organized society, and it is deeply affecting to walk among these sites in Bandelier National Monument area.

A week into my desert pilgrimage, I was invited to a party. Most of the guests were expatriates, working in the Southwest's booming media arts and computer industries. They came down from the northern rustbelt, or from Ontario and Quebec where things were flat, they said, and were creating a niche for themselves. Wherever I ventured, I met others like them, part of a youthful migration, giving up on California's earthquakes, fires and floods, on big-city entropy and drive-by shootings.

Some days later, I passed through the Phoenix area and while in Mesa wanted to get out into the desert for an afternoon. A poet friend said it was easy to find good birding territory: "Just walk to the edge of the houses where the bush begins across the street."

Following his advice, I headed south to Chandler and wheeled to the edge of a housing estate, found a drainage clearance through some private properties and cut across to an intense landscape. Arizona is a much different desert than Santa Fe: lusher, if that's the right word, more thickets and blooms. Phoenix is more cinematically an oasis town all the way around; the vegetation similar to the big island of Hawaii, but without the latter's enveloping jungle foliage: plenty of orchid creepers and palms. The valley desert was a carpet of blossoms and fervid with birds.

Within a short time, I'd spotted many lovely species, the Cactus Wren especially, state bird of Arizona, that nests in the enormous *Saguro* cactus. Then hiking up a series of sharp, crusty hills, I gained an amazing view of the whole country—a biblical-looking valley stretched vastly to the south and the east around me. It was rocky terrain, not well travelled, and to my astonishment I came across a faded petroglyph image, probably Ute.

Picking my way through the scree, I made for a final rock cropping, the highest point available before the next long escarpment. I pumped my way upward, keeping a keen eye out for rattlers. The terrain provided a natural sunning spot with many shady holes among the stones, and chattering ground squirrels looked fairly abundant. Reaching the point, I cleared a spot to rest free of thorn burrs when something struck at my face. Dumbstruck with terror, I recoiled only to laugh at my fears; inadvertently, terrifying both of us, I'd flushed a black-chinned hummingbird—locally uncommon, I read later—that whirred a mile a minute ten inches in front of my eyes.

It hit me then, both the rare bird and the spare naked beauty of the place, like a special gift from the desert Gods. I understand now why the desert seizes people's imaginations, and how, so often, they want to make a place for themselves there. It is a paradise in its own way, and always here with the historic culture of the aboriginals persistent in the background.

Slowly, gratefully, I made my way back down the hills.

1995

CUBA, FIDEL, AND CHE: HASTA LA VICTORIA, SIEMPRE!

CUBA

It is a truth universally acknowledged that travelling from Turtle Island—mainland North America—makes good sense during the winter months. Confirmation of this comes as you look out the window upon a snowy landscape not unlike Siberia. This year I had my customary Gauguin muse about seeing Tahiti, but almost immediately something floated up on the right-hand side of my computer screen: "Cuba..."

Cuba's U.S.-style consumer idea of progress screeched to halt in 1959, when rebel leader Fidel Castro, his brother Raul, and their remarkable guerrilla amigos, Che Guevara and Camilo Cienfuegos, overthrew the mafia-backed dictator Fulgencio Batista.

The U.S. trade embargo of more than fifty years has been ruinous to the island of eight million, and access to consumer goods of every sort remains sorely limited. Cuba comes with its share of bumps for independent travellers, but it's an unforgettable country. Its Varadero peninsula, a two-and-a-half-hour drive northeast of Havana, still welcomes most visitors with superb white sand beaches and all-inclusive resorts. Originally designed as a segregated tourist area with a controlled bridge-road access, it has a good airport and enough funky, busy tourist-strip attractions for most folks to settle into. As tourism is now central to the island's economy, new opportunities keep opening up, and this is a country worth further adventures. Bear in mind that as a visitor you'll be shown hospitality of a kind that won't always be available to local folks.

We like to feel grounded in a new country, and a few days at Varadero allows you to acclimatize before heading into the capital. A retired English sea captain gave us our best Cuba travel pointers. "I sailed in and out of Cuba's old sugar ports as a young officer before and after the liberation," he said. "Always liked it there. Still do. They were a great bunch to work with. The only difference after Fidel took over was that the men who loaded the sugar had pistols tucked in their belts, protecting their revolution. I never minded.

"There are one or two older hotels in Varadero, nothing fancy," he added. "They're at the end of the beach. Not the all-inclusive lot. The kind you might like."

Think of a long sand-dune peninsula reaching twenty kilometres into the sparkling Caribbean with an unblemished foreshore free of plastic junk. Two or three streets run parallel to it with a transit system of classic American cars from the 1950s, buses, horse-drawn tourist carts, modern taxis, foreigners on noisy rented motorbikes, and any sort of wheeled conveyance that can stoke up a head of steam. The main road runs for miles past one hotel resort after another. Many are beautifully modern and serve every sort of clientele, but most offer package holiday deals attracting middle-income snowbirds, families, seniors, and giddy student groups anxious to get sozzled as quickly as possible. Bottles of island rum are as cheap as you like. And painted on walls and displayed on posters all over the place, the famous Korda photograph image of Che Guevara—a suitable reminder of why Cuba is different from everywhere else in the Caribbean: A real revolution took place here, and Blessed be, for a change the underdogs won. *Viva la revolución!*

Women are safe and can walk alone pretty well anywhere. People here share. It's common to see men and women with their bags standing by a clear patch of road, waiting for a lift. If you have room in your vehicle, it's a matter of citizenship to invite them aboard.

You might hear gripes that the food in Cuba isn't this or that. Well, be imaginative. The best places always take a little seeking out anywhere; it's good to ask the locals. Our first evening we were directed up a flight of stairs to a small tidy place that looked like the main room of a family flat. That's exactly what it was. Half a dozen small tables, a waiter, and a limited but promising menu. What they had on offer was attractive, even with prices in U.S. dollars. These *paladars*, or private family places, have become common as part of the government's liberalized tourism policy. Get inside; it'll be tasty. And in Cuba it's all free-range, organic. There aren't any fast-food outlets. Maybe that's what critics gripe about. Who wouldn't want a fresh filet of marlin or yellowtail tuna? Salads, rice, and black beans are standard fare, and always somebody's auntie has made one or two desserts, with excellent Cuban-grown coffee and the rum that any island based on sugarcane is bound to have in barrels.

The capital, Havana, is not too far off. The journey by Viyazul state-owned bus with modern Chinese-built coaches is economical. In Havana, typically you stay in people's homes—*Casa Particulares*—and this is the way to go. In *Vieja* or Old Havana, buildings are frequently several hundred years old, and a tsunami of guesthouse renovations has been underway for the past ten years. These private guesthouses convert rooms and bathrooms within a large older family home, and the owners become entrepreneurs. Even if a property looks drab outside, many interiors are dramatic, even stunning.

Havana's ambiance is still resonant with the glamour of the Spanish Main. You can't enter this city either without a frisson of emotion at its revolutionary history: This is the town that cocked a snook at bullies everywhere and has lived to tell the tale. It's almost 500 years old and looks it. Packed with superb colonial architecture, *Habana Vieja* banks in close to the main harbour, and like most Cuban towns, this district is steadily crumbling away, so renovating it is a constant undertaking. The economic blockade has had a woeful impact. Much of Havana's colonial architecture was irreparable for lack of materials and is in advanced deterioration. Practically everything, even sand, has to be imported at costly expense, so most Cubans do without. People have to live somewhere though, a patchwork of buildings in good and bad repair alike line the streets, walls often held up by jerry-built props of heavy timber. It's a city where balconies routinely collapse after heavy rains.

As we shambled near the waterside one hot afternoon, this became clear. Four or five men were restoring the interior of a church that had fallen into disrepair. Inside, a labourer mixed mud—mortar—for two masons on a scaffold. I nodded. He exchanged the greeting. "*Mi padre era un albañil,*" I said. My father was a stonemason.

"*Bueno! Y tu tambien?*" You too?

"*Non, yo soy un escritor,* a writer." I stepped inside and watched him slurrying mortar with his shovel. We'd used a one-to-three mix, masonry cement and sand. Smooth, not too runny or stiff. His mud box looked runny. The dry cement looked all right. It was the sand. I took a quick look at a pile nearby and ran a little through my fingers. It wasn't talcum, but not far off. Good mortar needs coarse river sand to bond with cement. The men were using beach sand, soft white stuff. Not nearly enough strength in it to last. It's why the old walls collapse. My father would have been dismayed seeing hard workers without the right material for the job. On an island surrounded by sandy beaches, even building sand is imported from Brazil. For decades the Cubans were denied even this.

The United Nations has stepped in and is steadily helping refurbish the grandest old plazas and buildings. How many of these old landmarks would have resisted gentrification without the blockade is a provocative question. How many would have been demolished and rebuilt during the past fifty years if corporate ethics had ruled here, making way for chain hotels, Kentucky Fried Chicken, or Starbuck's corner locations? In a weird turnabout, the embargo has had some heritage benefits, helping save this historic city for the world. Mind you, tell that to the poor Cubans who have had nothing of the flow of commerce that would have brought them more food, clothing, better shelter, more comfort, more toys, more junk—the yin and yang of open-market trading.

The economic blockade which prevented new American cars from entering Cuba resulted in the preservation of thousands of pre-1959 Detroit-built vehicles. The roads here are museums—Batmobiles with giant tail fins and acres of gleaming chrome tool about the streets, and every kind of funky collector car rents itself out as a taxi. Cuban ingenuity in making replacement parts keeps the cars going well past their normal life span. Every day around Revolution Square, you see their owners touching up and shining these maximumly cool machines.

In Havana there's always a party going on after sundown. "You been here long?" Jorge, the first waiter we met in a café, asked. Jorge spoke decent English, and it took minutes to establish his role as a fixer. With subdued finesse, he made sure we ate well, ran up a little bill for the house, before directing us back to our lodgings easily. Naturally, he set us up the following day with a roaring-red convertible and driver— his "cousin," Ricardo.

We met Jorge and Ricardo on a neutral corner and spent the next eight hours doing the town on a Sunday.

"You a writer? Then you know Ernesto Hemingway. Let's go!"

"We thought to see a few places in town—the John Lennon monument, the Casa de las Américas, it's a cultural centre..."

"Oh sure, we gonna see all that. But first Ricardo and me gonna take you driving up the Malecon. You know, beside the ocean? Then we drive by the old Mafia hotels in Vedado. Great for pictures. It's where they got showgirls again at night. You want tickets?"

We didn't, and only goofs embark without a guidebook of some sort. Read up on where you're headed. Learn some history, a handful of handy phrases—Where's the toilet, please? We'd plotted out a route, and the Malecon seafront and the old Mafia hotels were on it. So were a few grand old embassy houses, then Revolution Square with its giant Che and Camilo Cienfuegos murals. Ricardo wore a natty little Frank Sinatra brim and was an obliging driver. Jorge was the negotiator. He knew the ropes, and he knew his clientele: forget the flamingo dancers. "Okay, my amigos, we gonna see the historic buildings but not really enter on this hot day. First, let's go John Lennon."

Fidel didn't like the Beatles. Cubans were building a revolution and didn't have time for rock 'n' roll fluff. Later on, Fidel said in an interview that he'd got that part of the sixties wrong. So, in a leafy district within a small park surrounded by houses, he established a memorial with an admirable statue of Lennon, a revolutionary sort of musician in his own regard. Ricardo parked in the shade, and we walked to the statue, Lennon relaxing on a bench. People keep snitching his round eyeglasses, so there's an elderly caretaker who'll bring along a spare set for picture-taking. The Lennon shrine, as it has become, is a nice place to gear down, even move through a little Tai Chi with no one to bother you.

Vedado is Havana's stylish district with the city's only really large hotels and the embassies. But Jorge's deal was to get us to some outlaying places we'd likely not make on our own.

"You know Cojimar, this village, right?" Jorge queried. "Where Hemingway he wrote *The Old Man and the Sea*. Still a good place, not too busy. Ricardo lives here, so we make a visit to La Terraza while he sees his family. It's the bar where Hemingway worked plenty."

Up and down, around, bump, hang on. And there we were. A vintage bar-restaurant above the bay. "Look at those boats on the beach," Jorge pointed. That's where Hemingway went fishing."

We saw plenty of evidence of Hem around the place. Loads of photos on the wall, the novelist front and centre, and his boat exactly as Jorge pointed out. The place was worn and scuffed enough to feel authentic, because that's exactly what it was. You can run up a tab in downtown Havana at other places where Hemingway liked to drink, but in Cojimar there's an authenticity to his presence that your granny's bulldog couldn't shake. Surprisingly, only a few other visitors dropped by that afternoon. They'd heard about Hemingway, of course, but had paid a lot more for the ride—three of them, middle-aged Korean women, and they didn't care what it cost. Besides, they'd just landed a free translator. They wanted a good time and started buying drinks with real élan.

"They're saying they wanted to see Cuba before the Americans come back and wreck the place," Kwan-shik translated. "Hemingway is a big deal for them. Us Koreans love literature, right? So they'd like to buy us a big shot of rum."

Cojimar is precisely as you'd want your literary experience. Memorable, edgy enough to keep you alert after a couple of mojitos in the early afternoon. "It's *Hemingwayesque*," I proposed.

"Who?" Jorge asked.

"Hemingway—*Papa* Ernesto..."

"Oh sure, he was a big guy in this La Terraza place. And he like drinking this *ron* too!"

We'd always thought Ron Bacardi was a guy's name, not simply Bacardi *rum*. So much for high-school Spanish. With Jorge near to hand, the stories kept coming. So did the music when Ricardo turned up with three *cantadores* in pillowy red shirts he knew from the neighbourhood who promptly, sensing big tips, started singing and strumming for the Korean *señoras*.

"This is turning out to be fun," Kwan-shik said, grinning. "Hiring Ricardo and his gangster car is a great investment—we're shelling out $30 for the whole day with a car and our two protectors. These gals from Taegu are forking out $25 per hour, and they'll be in for a couple of hundred, but it's exciting. When they get home, they'll go back to being proper *mama-sans.*"

"What happens in Havana stays in Havana..."

Havana's pedestrian-only Calle Obispo is one of the most finger-snapping streets on Earth. It doesn't get cooler than this. Narrow, packed with strolling couples, wild art galleries, boutiques, open-air cafés one after the other with swinging rumba combos and great prices. Lobster dinners, chilled Cuban beer, and top-quality rum and cigars everywhere. You can have fun all night for twenty bucks and there's a lot of living here for free. Outside a café one Sunday evening, we passed a young man singing, just him and his guitar. Seated on a rattan chair in the street, he looked like a movie star, singing with the voice of an angel that brought a thrill to the heart. A block away in the old plaza, an old black musician sat in the shade of a colonial palazzo, dressed in vintage threads—white suit, black shirt, two-tone shoes, hipster tie, and a sharp Panama—Buena Vista Social Club, right? He played bluesy trumpet in the night, not worried who listened, an aging young rebel blowing beneath the stars.

In Havana you join the revolution and drink rum; and even if you don't smoke, you learn how to smoke a cigar. *Viva la revolución!*

We met a Pole who told us about the music that all the bands played. "That song they're singing, can you understand it?" he asked, reaching over from his chair at the next table. "'*Hasta Siempre Comandante.*' It's about Che Guevara...faithful until the end."

Rum helps with speaking a little Spanish. I added a few notes to the band's thank-you hat and asked if they'd sing it again. They didn't mind singing it again at all, and straight away the crowded café was singing along too. It made sense to stay in this friendly place for a while.

"Peace in the world tonight, amigos..." Our new Polish friend looked beatific.

Our band kept on swaying and swinging with a sax and a pretty girl on flute. Next door another combo laid down constant grooves with two handsome singers and a version of Cuban R & B; up the lane it was three guitars like the Gypsy Kings. These artists were smart. Every band on the street had a different sound and look—they don't compete against each other. The whole street works to keep it grooving. Even the cops are friendly.

When the starry nights end and the sun rolls around again, art and book aficionados share similar rich harvests. Thoroughfares and side streets of the old town are packed with galleries, often the ground floor of a house or apartment, and you can afford their wares, with the proviso that on departure you'll need to purchase an export license: it's a paperwork exercise to plan for. A stroll after coffee presents the city's literary associations. Plinths and statues honour Miguel de Cervantes, Portugal's *Lusiad* poet Luis de Camões, and others. In the old quarter, the upscale Ambos Mundos hotel has a whacking collection of Hemingway memorabilia; the novelist worked here during the thirties on *For Whom the Bell Tolls.* Daytime, around the Plaza de Armas, built in 1520 and still attractive, booksellers hawk collectibles. Early Che Guevara publications in cheap paper run a couple of dollars; their revolutionary-era illustrations worth framing. In January it's Havana's International Book Fair at San Carlos Cabaña Fortress across the harbour. The annual bash tours through the country and features a major *salon du livre* with poetry readings, seminars on Latin American authors, children's activities, and art exhibitions.

Three hours southwest of the capital by road, you reach Viñales in Pinar del Rio Province.

Due to the blockade, the Viñales Valley survives as an exquisitely unique preindustrial farming region—perhaps 150 square kilometres of mountain-enclosed, small family-owned farms under intensive red-earth agriculture. The range of crops here would bring tears of joy to the eyes of a greengrocer—sugarcane, coffee, manioc tapioca, pineapples, greenleaf vegetables, and an abundance of succulent fruits. Roam around the countryside, and you'll see healthy pigs and chickens free all over. The surrounding peaks lend majesty, but the most dramatic topographical features are the strange *mogotes*, freestanding calcified limestone monoliths that have been shaped over eons by rain and wind; they lend a surreal element to an already tranquil landscape. It can feel as if you're in a lost world here. The valley's lush, over-ripe fields are essentially all organic since farmers have had no access to commercial fertilizers or pesticides for decades. Oxen still plow these fields, and crops are sown by hand, then weeded and harvested by hand and machete. People work hard.

The town of under 30,000 is low-rise and tidy. The main drag leads north to Havana. It's another friendly place, without hassles, lazy enough that you don't mind stopping in the shade and having a cold beer at practically any hour to watch the world pass by. The generous number of restaurants and decent bars, for a place its size, suggests there's a reliable stratum of backpacker action going on. In daylight, scattered vendors set up tables—the region's wood-carvers are particularly talented in Pinar del Rio. It's a good community for a walkabout, and we found some of the best food in the country.

Hitting town on the bus, we found hawkers waiting at the stop, advertising rooms and rates. Casa particulars in Viñales are relatively basic, although a few have invested and gone further upscale with a swimming pool. Otherwise, rooms are a typical add-on to the back of the family home, with your own compact shower and toilet. The latter amenities are needed by law. Marketing to tourists has become important to the economy; however, Cuba's Socialist/Communist system makes stiff demands on the operators of private rooms. Our landlady clarified this one evening as she walked us up for a look at her enormous pig in a cage on a very small allotment. *Casa* operators are obliged to remit a specified fee to the authorities each month whether they are able to chalk it up from visitors or not, and the fee is not negligible.

Viñales townsite is fairly level, and walking about is easy; go-getters can rent bicycles. The universal reason for heading here though is for walking the valley's peaceful hills.

"Do you go trekking in the valley?" our young landlady asked. We indicated that was indeed our ambition. "You can have a guide to show you the best places," she suggested.

Half an hour later, a young man from close by called in to meet us. Luis proposed to guide us the next day on a walk in the foothills and through the superbly green tobacco croplands. If we were happy, we could go out with him again the following day.

And so at nine the following morning, we set off, the church bell clanging up the lane as we walked to the centre of town where a hot blue '56 Dodge waited on us. It was only a short whiz to our embarkation point, but worth it. If you only cruise to a place once in your life, why not in a set of wheels that Jack Kerouac and Neil Cassady would have been proud to joyride for kicks? Then we were off, pleasant in the morning freshness.

We hiked with Luis past many small farms, people never failing to wave and call out hello. One man stood over a low charcoal fire, stirring something steadily with a long pole in what looked like a large metal hubcap. "What's he doing?" I inquired.

"Roasting coffee beans." He pointed up a slope. "Those are his trees." Then he waved and we carried on.

Despite the humble living conditions, each small *finca* or farmstead had precisely one modest-sized solar panel placed on the ground near the house. The panels appeared inexplicably out of place in this undeveloped area. "A French scientist came to work here," Luis said. "He liked the people of the valley and gave every family one of these panels as a gift. Maybe from his country, I don't know. We can use them for small appliances and basic computers. Even some light in the evening. It's very useful. I learned English on my computer."

A short time later, while enjoying the company of three brothers he knew and one of their entrancingly beautiful wives in baggy work pants and rubber boots, Luis gestured acknowledgment to his friends, saying, "Farmers in this valley can support themselves with food. They grow enough to sell in small town markets too. We can do that now, except for the tobacco." Even for nonsmokers, it's a beautiful sight to look out on fields of leafy tobacco. Small and supple, the leaves had thrown me off.

Why, I can't say, but I'd somehow believed that tobacco leaves were thick and broad, arm's-length wide. In Viñales the leaves are almost too lovely to think of picking, running in tidy fields that follow the contours of the land.

"This is the best tobacco land in the world, where the famous Cohiba and Monte Cristo cigars come from," Luis explained for us as we walked back on the trail. "The government maintains a monopoly on tobacco because it produces wealth for Cuba. Farmers have to sell ninety per cent of their crops to the state, that's the law."

"What about the rest?"

"They can sell the other ten per cent to visitors or in markets. Their fields and methods are very productive. If you like, we can visit the drying sheds to see how the cigars are made. But first, we can taste some coffee that my mother will make for you. This is our family house."

He gestured toward a small house, a cottage surrounded by fruit and coffee trees at the back toward higher ground. Chickens clucked, and a sleek-looking pig snuffled beneath the trees, rooting for windfalls. In the little house, a polite country mother welcomed us in Spanish and led us to a small, handmade table and chairs. A crucifix and image of the Madonna with a tiny candle had a place before a photograph. "My father," Luis nodded. The room was unadorned otherwise, except for several paintings. "My work," Luis said of his landscapes. A plate of bananas appeared. Then Luis's mother brought us coffee in small cups. "My mother says to you this coffee is from our own trees," our young guide said, smiling. It was of excellent quality, fragrant the way that coffee tastes in Jamaica's Blue Mountains or the highlands in Bali. "My mother roasts this herself," Luis nodded proudly. "It's better than that fellow's we saw from the road… "

Kwan-shik reached out her hand. "Does your mother sell this coffee? Would she have any we could take home to Canada? Can you ask?"

Luis rattled softly in Spanish. His mother looked embarrassed and turned her head. "She doesn't like to say it to you, but we can give you some."

"We'd like to buy it, *por favor*. It's like a privilege for us to receive it from the family that grows it. When we invite our friends back home in for coffee like this, we can tell them the story of how we met you and your mother in Viñales."

With two pounds each in our light daypacks, we said goodbye and set off again, a satisfying weight on our backs. Up and down, around and across ridges, we wandered, past fields and meadows, horses and cattle. Occasionally a banged-up old jalopy or obsolete Russian army truck loaded with produce or hay and people going or coming from town might pass, but most travel is on horseback here, or a pony or ox cart. Bicycles are highly treasured, Luis remarked. "Canadians bring them for touring, then leave them behind or exchange for their room and board, so we have a little steady supply." He laughed, hunching his shoulders at this little bit of fortune that could arrive in the valley.

Call it the devilment, but I wondered about the farmers we passed. Were they really content? "The government here," I asked Luis, "how do people feel about it? The revolution was more than fifty years ago. There are problems…"

True to his nature, Luis was upfront. "The people here prefer the revolution. We got problems, but not like before. My father told me about before Fidel times—if the *jefes*, the bosses, liked your horse, they just took it. Nothing you could do. They had the power. They could take your daughter. We *don't* go back."

"*Verdad?*" True?

"You can ask anybody. We don't all want live in Miami."

That evening over a beer in town, we agreed to go out with Luis again next day. Something about Viñales starts calling.

Cave exploring in the national ecological preserve here is more or less expected. Luis urged us to walk to the lengthy cave structures of Santo Tomás. They extend more than forty kilometres, but a sensible half-mile stretch of pitch-black, stumbling spooky fun is about the limit for most non-vampires. There you are, with only the scantiest of guide lights, surrounded by limestone stalactites and stalagmites. In the dark, I remembered the voice of my geography professor articulating the difference between the two: "When the mites go up, the tights come down!"

In the blackness, a pair of Swiss girls bumbled about on their own, and out of solidarity, we invited them to join us. Luis had sensibly rented a little lantern from a farmer, otherwise we'd have been as hooped as Plato's cave squatters in *The Republic*. Then, amazingly, like a science-fiction dream, at the very end of the route, we came upon an underground pool of pure mountain water. It was brisk. We looked at each other in the faint glimmer of light. The solution was obvious. We stripped off, and four foreigners swam together naked in the blackness, save for Luis's eerie little lantern, on our own in the obscurity of a 50,000-year-old cave. Strange boyhood shivers hit me. It felt like a monster could crash up from the water any second. That evening we ate lamb's neck stew and dumplings with extra tots of rum to warm up.

In recent years, a small number of boats have begun passenger operations, and you might land a passage if you schmooze about the docks off Havana's central plaza. Santiago in the mountainy Oriente region lies to the starboard or eastern side of the island, due north of Jamaica and not far off Haiti to the southeast. The heartland of Cuba's substantial Afro-Cuban culture, the city has established literary and revolutionary credentials. In the 1950s, Graham Greene worked on his comic Cold War novel, *Our Man in Havana,* while taking in the shady terrace hospitality of the central Hotel Casa Grande. The similarities between its main terrace overlooking the Parque Cespedes and Saigon's Hotel Continental where he worked on his moral and political masterwork *The Quiet American* are inescapable.

Rebellion and intrigue run in this town's blood. Greene, a wartime intelligence officer, wrote that every man, woman, and child in Santiago supported Fidel's rebels during their struggle. A short distance from the Casa Grande, you come upon the Moncada Barracks where Castro's small guerrilla force launched their second revolution in the 1950s. It's now a school.

We made a point of hiring a driver who assured us he had "a good American car" to get us out of Santiago. Naturally he turned up in a battered Russian Lada. It should have been no surprise. This city is home to the nation's real hustlers. You need steely determination to shake off the street jive that can emerge here. But we wanted to see the Sierra Maestra mountains; this is where Fidel and eighty revolutionary fighters holed up after slipping in from Mexico aboard the *Granma* in '56. This is where their history-changing revolution came from. It is quiet and very hot in the hills, but worth the effort to freelance a little and get out there. In our rumbling junk-heap, we climbed slowly higher into the hills, passing military camps or depots that are otherwise only rarely encountered here, certainly less so than in, say, Mexico. The equipment we saw looked dated, well used, for an army, I reckoned, that must run on soul.

The Basilica of Neustra Señora del Cobre, Cuba's holiest shrine, is also situated in these mountains in a verdant little valley. It's a lovely airy cathedral. John Paul the Polish pope who was no friend of communism came here during his historic visit in 1998 and was embraced by Fidel. The night before they launched their revolution, the mother of Fidel and Raul went there, too, to pray for her sons: Liberation and faith have complex, entwined history in this land.

In a very poor country, you see faith up close. At El Cobre, it's there in the piles of cast-off crutches, left there after *miraculos*; and it's in the glass cases in the basilica—in another atheist Cuban Communist irony, every unit and division of their armed forces has its badges and insignias on display here. You see it in the towering white statue of Christ the Redeemer that rises above Havana harbour, not as colossal as Rio, but still imposing. "Why were we never told of these things, only about the beards and the commie bad stuff instead?" I asked myself aloud. Why weren't we told that the first thing tossed in the trash after Havana's liberation was the American Mafia that ran the capital as a private playground? Why hadn't we heard that Che Guevara lived four doors down the lane from the Redeemer above the harbour after the revolution? Who covered it up?

Journeying to a proper old pirate stronghold, better do it by boat. Punta Frances at the western edge of *Isla de la Juventud*, the Island of Youth, is a pristine ecological preserve that offers a view of what Europeans must first have glimpsed in the Caribbean. Despite many name changes, it endures in imagination as the inspiring source of Robert Louis Stevenson's beloved *Treasure Island.* The waters adjacent were the hunting grounds of French buccaneer Jean Latrobe, who raided vessels and purportedly buried the loot of two Spanish galleons in this remote beach area, a massive gold hoard that has never been found. The island itself was not prized by Spanish-era overlords and mumbled along as a marginal agricultural fief. It has fine beaches everywhere, yet the isle's claim to fame is more dubious: Fifty kilometres across the Gulf of Batabanó from mainland Cuba, it made an ideal prison. Fidel himself, with the followers of his first failed insurrection, was jailed here from 1953 to 55. Ferries and a hodgepodge of vessels work out of Cienfuegos, and we arrived at daybreak to serene sapphire-blue water and a beach with blinding white coral sand and a soft ring of coconut palms—the poster image for every runaway dream you've known.

There is one creaky wooden jetty where smaller tenders can chug you ashore from a larger boat, and that's it. Now it's just you and the pelicans, the water teeming with fast sleek fish just a few feet offshore. You simply set off walking up the sand into paradise. This environmental wonder is another curious bonus from the blockade, held off from almost certain free-market tourist despoliation. That's the odd thing about Cuba. Communist, it resembles nothing I can ever recall from the iron-fisted regimes I saw in Eastern Europe back in the hard Cold War days. Neighbourhood Communist Party offices here usually look pretty dilapidated. Somewhere there'll be a photograph of Fidel, but in the main, curiously out of sight.

"It's Che who's everywhere; he's a secular saint," I remarked, as we got ready for home our last afternoon.

"Of course, don't you see? Che is always young—he died early," Kwan-shik said. "Fidel grew old and white-haired, but Che is always vibrant and brave, so the image of the revolution is always young." So it is in Cuba, this place of constant discovery. *Hasta la Victoria siempre!*

2015

WRESTLING WITH TIME

東京

TOKYO

Fury supplies the weapons.

—Virgil, *The Aeneid*

Staying with friends in Tokyo recently, I spoke with Shogo Oketani, the literary translator, about life in Vancouver as an immigrant kid during the fifties and early sixties. Oddly, as it turned out, professional wrestling played a big part in both our boyhoods, East and West.

Back then, however, we didn't think much about Asia. Europe was our cultural home. At school we sang anthems to the English Queen, saluted the Red Ensign and the Union Jack, and were obliged to mumble a Protestant version of the Lord's Prayer. Europe was the curbstone of history—English history—and we learned that the scarlet spread of Britain's dominions blanketed a quarter of the globe, including Canada from sea to shining sea.

Naturally, unspoken divisions existed. In New Westminster, where my family settled on emigration in 1957, prosperous families lived atop Massey Heights or overlooking Queen's Park, where, as youngsters, we danced the Maypole each spring. Portuguese and Italians lived in semi-rural Queensborough and along Burnaby's Trapp Road with their roadside ditches, nanny goats, and—in autumn—the heady odour of fermenting grapes. Greasers drag-raced there on Friday nights, and in summer kids drowned or were miraculously saved from the Fraser River's treacherous eddies after diving from log booms.

Maillardville's French-Canadians—at that time the only group privileged with hyphenated status—mainly worked in sawmills along the river and were good log boom men with their long peavey poles. They were Catholic, so the Irish crowd we knew mixed with them occasionally, and the French moms introduced us to *omelettes* after our First Holy Communion procession. The war had only been over for ten years or so, and feelings were still touchy about Germans and Italians; CKNW radio still regularly played foreign songs like "Sailor Sailor," "Volare," and "Dominique." Religion remained a powerful force though; at church-hall dances, immigrants could waltz and date across old antagonisms, and that was how people got to be friends again.

In the late fifties, all along the Fraser from Steveston to Mission, big house parties provided the action upstairs and downstairs. As kids we piled into whatever space wasn't being used by the grownups. These were golden days with taxis full of sailors and English officers invited up from ships in port. Everyone jived and drank Barbados ship's rum and Coca-Cola.

House parties were always an adventure, like the UN, everyone mixing and courting. Older kids usually led us up the stairs from the basement to peek through the door at what was going on. Country and western music and Elvis would be bouncing from the hi-fi as our mothers smoked cigarettes and danced with the sailors. The priest would be in the kitchen with the whiskey, and our dads poured drinks. Sooner or later we'd be called on to show everyone how to dance the Twist, then they'd shift us downstairs again with sodas, and that was how we learned what it was like to throw a party.

New Westminster back then had just one Afro-Canadian family. A number of Chinese families kept corner stores and restaurants about the town, and a smaller number of Japanese could be met at school. Because we knew families where fathers and uncles had been cruelly treated as prisoners in the Far East, hard feelings remained about the Japanese, wherever they came from—nobody talked about the wartime internment back then—and the after-school cartoon programs kept up lurid images of Asian otherness. That's what made Kinji Shibuya such a terrifying wrestling star.

In those boyhood days, sports heroes loomed larger than life. Every fall, the BC Lions ruled Vancouver. Through the winter, we faithfully followed Flying Phil Maloney and the Pacific Coast League's Canucks hockey squad. But year in, year out, presteroid professional wrestling was where, for seventy-five cents, a kid and his best friend could see it all won and lost in the ring every Friday night. There's no describing our adulation for a hero like Mr. Kleen, or our rage at Edmonton roughneck Gene Kiniski. This stuff was real, we knew that in our bones. Every immigrant knew it, and the promoters ensured every ethnic group had a guy to cheer for—Hungarian? Sandor Kovacs. German? Eric Froelich—a "scientific" wrestler. Irish? Terrible Tommy O'Toole and Roy McClarty. Latino? Hercules Cortes. Slavic? Killer Kowalski. Viking Bob Morse, Chief Crazy Horse, Tex MacKenzie... Bad guys, good guys, someone for everyone, and we saw them all. And when one round of heroes faded, in came the wrestling midgets, the battling Amazons led by the one and only Fabulous Moolah, or the big guy, Haystack Calhoun—all topped by the inevitable, mysterious Masked Man, Mr. X. For a kid forty-odd years ago, it didn't get more real than that.

Then Kinji Shibuya came to town. A short, sneaky jujitsu artist with a sharp little goatee and just enough English to outrage local wrestling fans, overnight he became the most hated and feared star of the local wrestling circuit, the living incarnation of evil for us die-hard fans. Shibuya conquered every man before him. He also had the theatrics down pat, pushing every red-hot button in the showman's repertoire. Within weeks, the threat of him alone could turn the Friday night father-and-son faithful of the local Queens Park Arenex into a screaming army looking for a saviour, a real Canadian to knock the sneer off Mr. Shibuya.

Gene Kiniski—self-proclaimed "Canada's Greatest Athlete"—was long known as the dirtiest, raunchiest, pre-Shibuya cuss in the business. But when the Japanese terror had wiped the floor with every good guy in local Christendom, by default alone it was left to Kiniski, former terror of the meek, to take on the demon Kinji Shibuya and whup him once and for all—preferably in each Lower Mainland and Vancouver

Island wrestling market. And when Mitsu Arakawa, Kinji's Tokyo cousin showed up in town to help him clean up the tag-team wars, there was only one other body-basher ornery enough to join up with Kiniski in the mayhem—to turn back the Yellow Horde—and the promoters didn't spare the horses in bringing him in from Boston—well, from Alberta as it later turns out—Hard-Boiled Haggerty, Fighting Irishman extraordinaire and *personal friend* of the Kennedy family.

He had the proof. There on the Saturday Old Dutch Potato Chip-sponsored All-Star Wrestling broadcast live from BCTV studios on Lougheed Highway, with host Ron Morrier and men's haberdashery advertiser Fred Asher looking on, Hard-Boiled Haggerty with his missing teeth showed us all a framed photo portrait of himself and the two beloved Kennedy brothers, John Fitzgerald and Bobby Francis. It was like he'd been personally blessed by the pope.

You know the final outcome. But there I was in Tokyo, telling my friend Shogo that this is what it felt like back then. He understood too. In Japan they'd had the same kind of deal, he said, only in reverse, a blonde American giant who whupped every Japanese scrapper until there was only one last honourable samurai, Rikidozan, who could save the nation's honour, what was left of it, after the holocaust of the war. The ultimate combat happened all over again every time these guys hauled themselves into the ring. Okay, so he was really Kim Sin-Nak, a North Korean *Zainichi* and not the Nagasaki hard rock every kid idolized, only this time, the good guys won both sides of the Pacific. Such dreams mythologies are built on. After all, our kids have to learn that somehow the good guys really can win, as unlikely as that can sound these days. But then, as a wise old Dutchman once told me, "If you want to know what's happening in the daily news, read Plato."

Somehow, it all seems more than a little like *Bye Bye Brazil.* But then everything changed one day. Along came the Beatles.

2008
NEW WESTMINSTER

LA FRANCE TOUJOURS LA FRANCE

My Granny once told me the French soldiers that fought beside my Grandad at the Battle of the Somme in WWI were very brave. For a boy this was important; usually the French got slagged, especially for eating frog's legs. When I began reading in earnest, a tale in my favourite school book told the story of the Fête des Filets Bleus, a Breton fishing boat festival at Concarneau. So on finally reaching Paris as a young man, while I knew only rags and tags about Sartre and Existentialism, I'd already learned a particle or two about the spirit of France and her people.

After the requisite tourist stops during short visits to Paris as a student, I walked its streets, such as the Avenue Cardinal Lemoine, using Ernest Hemingway's *A Moveable Feast* as my guide. This furnished me with a romantic education; the artists and writers had all been there—impressionists, postimpressionists, Scott Fitzgerald, Gertrude Stein, Henry Miller, James Joyce. The world of arts and letters had revolved around the City of Light for a century, and many of the great locations where it had flourished could still be seen—the Café Select, the Closerie des Lilas, Shakespeare and Company, the Moulin Rouge. You can still call into them; however, bring your credit card to most. Once, I made a chilly winter visit to the cemetery at Montparnasse to visit the graves of poets Guillaume Apollinaire and Paul Verlaine—"literary graving," they call it—a pastime I've indulged in many places ever since.

Getting to the world's most popular travel destination is a matter of choice. From London you've got the Chunnel Train—after boarding at Waterloo you can be standing at the Gare du Nord three and a half hours later. Or for roughly the same money, you can go by regular rail and a ninety-minute ferry crossing and celebrate en route to Paris with a comfortable hotel and a night on the town in Calais. Either way, the Normandy countryside rolls evenly out the window, horizon to horizon. To your northeast will be the Great War's front-line trench areas where my grandfather fought, and where Al Neil, Canada's wildest artist and jazz *bon vivant* from Vancouver, battled through with the Royal Canadian artillery after D-Day.

At first glance, Calais may look unprepossessing. There's plenty in the provinces. Life is calmer here than in the capital, and prices more forgiving. The Flemish architecture of the town hall is elegantly imaginative, and Rodin's universally admired public sculpture, *The Burghers of Calais,* is overpowering in its indictment of the horrors of war. Walk on to the central Place d'Armes, select a restaurant for dinner—mostly seafood, and relax into your journey with a proper glass of plonk; let the staff help you decide. The French know about these things.

It's all about eating in France, what Leonard Cohen called "the mouth culture." On a blowy night, a piping-hot onion soup with its toasted cheese lid is irresistible. Or the famous set-price *plats du jour* meals are always a bargain. A hearty repast for two might present, say, your soup, a bucket of mussels in garlic-herb broth or filet of haddock in white sauce *aux fines herbes*, salad, a basket of good bread, coffee, and crème caramel. *Vive la France!*

French *joie de vivre* isn't all the can-can and popping corks. After a fine meal, a sea-breeze stroll back to your room and some happy rest will have you arriving in Paris in better shape next day. The morning train rocks on via Lille, once the powerhouse centre of the Flanders linen trade, and there's a history lesson outside the window all the way where the poppies still grow. The Calais-Lille-Paris run is a soft ride in fine coaches and passes many small towns entirely French in character; you'll be deepening your familiarity with what it means to be in France. On our latest run, the conductress was young, long-haired, and buxom in a country way, dressed in a pantsuit uniform, mushroom-coloured with red trim, and wearing a cute *kepis*, like an off-duty Catherine Deneuve playing a Legionnaire. At every station stop, she stepped onto the platform, waited for the on and offs, took out her whistle and gave it a stylish blow like something out of *Dr. Zhivago. Et voilà…*

With the ructions over Britain's leaving the European Community, one wonders if the political protagonists in Westminster ever actually stopped for a look at Calais. During a ramble along the seafront road designed specifically for huge eighteen-wheel lorries hauling cargoes to and from the continent, you witness an unceasing flow of massive rigs from France, Italy, Spain, Bulgaria, Germany, Turkey, Poland, and so on, all heading for Dover and London—an eye-popping testament to the vast interwoven trading network between the U.K. and Europe.

But it's in Paris where an education in art appreciation and culture unfolds organically, starting with any comfortable café *terrace* where you can dust off that high-school French and plump up your *savoir faire*. My own first walkabouts in this City of Light were among the shabby streets of Montmartre, then on to the impressionist painters and their postimpressionist followers at the Jeu de Paume. Housed now in the Musée D'Orsay on the Left Bank of the Seine, this colossus of the creative imagination cannot be left unseen. Backing up those early nights were sessions at La Cigalle, where Guadeloupe's Al Lirvat played tailgate trombone with his swinging band in Pigalle. An abundance of cheap hotels made it possible. Paris remains the most affordable great metropolis in the world; to this day you can cop budget digs near the beating heart of the city's main cultural precincts.

Even so, and although it is incandescently beautiful in many separate but conjoined fashions, because Paris is big, raw, and fabulous with its own burden to hump in the world, for a long time I struggled to like this city. Time, experience, age, friends, and a little more security can change all that.

Travel journeys are not unlike making love. You have the awe and emotional intensity of discovering a wonderful place for the first time.

Then you experience the grace of sharing what you've learned, and of introducing others to this wonderment. On a journey to France with my family, we took a little hotel in the Latin Quarter recommended by a friend in London. "You'll like it," she declared. "An ancient wobbly place, all exposed beams, rickety this and that, little rooms up the winding stairs. Good value, tucked just off Place Saint-Michel, 200 yards from Nôtre-Dame.

"Go downstairs for breakfast," she added. "It's always the same: crusty baguettes and jam—mind your teeth—and all the good coffee you can drink."

She left unsaid that we'd be in the city's old Left Bank nexus, full of life and surrounded by galleries, the best cheap restaurants, and jazz clubs, with all the colour and history of the Sorbonne a few streets away. Rue St.-André-des-Arts has been a magnet for visiting artists and wannabees since Fitzgerald and Hemingway wrote and drank themselves into fame here. Leopards don't change their spots. Our first morning, the hotel patron, a scholar of Proust, put down his book to converse, rattling off the names of French-Canadian and German authors who stayed regularly. "Are you *Americain*?" he inquired, lifting an eye in inspection.

"*Non, monsieur*. Canadian..."

"Becauze zere were ze Americain poets living just around ze corner. You passed ze old hotel zey lived in." He shrugged, puffing on a Gauloise. "I do some writing myself. On Proust, of course. Not published yet."

"Of course..."

I knew "the Beat Hotel." At 9 Git-le-Coeur, in a nearby alley, it was home to Jack Kerouac, my old teacher Allen Ginsberg, William Burroughs, and Gregory Corso in the fifties. Burroughs stayed on for years, collaborating with the artist Brion Gysin. And it was here, practically next door? *"Oui, monsieur."* After our book chat, the patron enjoyed having us, and our morning coffee sessions revealed him as an incorrigible gossip, with special jabs reserved for Sartre and de Beauvoir: *"Communistes,* all of zem," he said, pointing out the door. "Sartre drank his coffee on St. Germain out there. He had broken-women all over ze place. In ze war, ze Resistance never trusted him..."

"I'll keep that in mind..."

The *Boul'Mich* area is a squabble of narrow streets, jammed with shops and passersby. Students from the Sorbonne have flocked to its gallimaufry of Latin Quarter cafés for good cheap meals for hundreds of years. One of the city's oldest architectural precincts, its bohemian credentials still shine among its bookshops, galleries, and endlessly distracting memorabilia dealers. I led the family for a look at the Beat Hotel, now a boutique haunt for well-heeled travellers. A *plaque commémorative* on the wall outside harks to its association with Beat Generation writers. "It's a curious feeling to read a historic plaque when you've known, or met, some of these figures," I said to Kwan-shik. She winked, and with a tug at my pullover, we set off again. Already the kids were angling for a look at the neighbourhood's morning fruit market.

Practised travel philosophy advocates taking time to organize a schedule and make some lists; you can generally cover most sights you'd hope to see in most great cities in about three or four days. You begin by asking, What's important? What do I absolutely have to see? What do we need to share. As a strategy, it holds up for most of the visitor almanac's greatest hits, plus a few self-discoveries; if there's more, well, that's for next time.

Paris is magnificent. The skyline alone can absorb your attention for ages, especially at morning when the sun is rising and illuminating the whiteness of the city's great, magic hill, Montmartre, with its curious, oddly proportioned dome casting an all-seeing gaze across the city. At evening, *la crepuscule,* that peculiarly blue Parisian stretch before the last light fades to darkness, is haunting along the Seine and has been celebrated by poets since Baudelaire. Then there are the unexpected treasures—that first unforgettable sight of Nôtre-Dame before the fire with its towers and sacred beauty, its tragic legend of the Hunchback that even children love. A walk up the Seine past inviting bars and cozy restaurants brings you to the Musée D'Orsay where the sprawling impressionist collection is housed across the river from the Louvre. Here is Matisse, Toulouse-Lautrec, Degas, Van Gogh, Rodin's sculptures—an incomparable collection.

"I'll find Cezanne." Kwan-shik gestured with her museum brochure. "That's my guy." With our daughter, she set off for the protean genius and his canvases in praise of sunny Provence.

A metro stop takes you to the Arc de Triomphe, and with luck you'll catch an itinerant gypsy band in full-on Django swinging performance—always a blast. With our children beside us, we arrived one long summer's evening at six o'clock to a dignified military ceremony conducted by old soldiers in honour of their fallen comrades. It's a moving daily ritual. You stand beneath the huge arch emblazoned with Napolean's bewildering number of victories, though, in the way of big winners, nothing noted of Moscow, Leipzig, or Waterloo.

Depending on your level of waiting-line tolerance, the *Mona Lisa* at the Louvre is best approached late in the day. Early birds coalesce into heavy morning line-ups that last until mid-afternoon. At three o'clock, we dodged the line-ups, looking in on Leonardo's other bit of magic, *The Virgin of the Rocks,* and the broody Caravaggios en route to viewing da Vinci's enigmatic noblewoman. The guards certainly looked tired when we approached dear old Mona: "Imagine standing all day like that," our daughter repined, reflecting her own tired legs. The *Mona Lisa.* There she waits, on display with her controlled lighting. It's like meeting the Queen; you don't get much time with her, but now you've officially seen it.

The Louvre is wearying in size; right to the end, there's always one more room to see. Leaving, the sun was warm, and we cooled off our feet in the water pavilions and fountains, gazing upon the classical stonework of the palace. Paris lies all around you with her beckoning streets and glorious architecture. It's simply a matter of deciding which direction to follow.

Walking together along the riverside toward the Zen Centre near Place de la Bastille, we came upon a delicious sight, only in Paris. Beneath a tarp cover over his wooden cart stall, a man was selling fragrant sausages, heavy wheels of cheese, and exquisitely baked hearth loaves from the Auverne country, famed since Roman times for its food.

"*Bonjour*, would you like to try…?"

On impulse, we began sampling the tasty dried sausage with myrtille berries, purchasing a couple of fine lengths, then tried a sharp cheddar-type cheese sliced from a round of Cantal. *Scrumptious.* With a loaf of bread, we made a picnic and walked off to the side of the Seine. Our London friend had made us a gift of an unusual French knife, razor sharp, with a round wooden handle. "It's a market knife, for shopping, for peeling things, and so forth," she explained. "You'll see it's perfectly handy!" And it was, with a special locking switch to ensure the blade never springs against you. What an hour we spent on the grass, watching the canal boats passing by and smacking our lips.

At the Zen Centre, you are received into a private courtyard property, then at a second gated garden where a Korean Zen Master has purchased a house that manifests itself as an oasis of the dharma in the midst of a city. Invited to sit in family meditation in the zendo hall, we did our best to empty our minds and express our gratitude, an ideal moment of stillness, followed by tea with a pair of attendant monks. Kwan-shik asked in Korean, "May we ask you how the dharma is received here?"

"We find it is difficult offering Zen in Paris; the reception has been modest at best," a visiting monk responded.

"I wonder if it isn't because people here are already content," Kwan-shik said. At receiving this information, the monks nodded in somewhat bemused if awkward consideration.

If you've ever looked at Toulouse-Lautrec or seen Shirley MacLaine and Jack Lemmon in the hilarious *Irma La Douce*, you must pay respects to Montmartre, *naturellement*, if not for the artists and its fabled history, at least for a visit to the grand whiteness of Sacré-Coeur Basilica. What a view of the city from its steps! Historic Paris is still the most beautiful city in the world, and the vista from here is unrivalled—epic, sprawling, but always civilized. One never tires of it. And if a young gent were to wander down the steep steps toward a viewing of the fleshier entertainments in Pigalle, well, *c'est la vie, n'est-ce pas?* With its history of welcoming and nurturing great painters, Montmartre has always been a source of fascination. We noted how even more African and Arabic the area had become since our previous visits; then after giving Kwan-shik the high sign, the girls repaired to browsing the shops while I led my son off to naughty Pigalle for a walkabout. Ah, Pigalle! It was just as I recalled from my misspent youth—the cheesy peep show parlours and tawdry glamour of neon-lit striptease bars, tired-looking Lebanese and Turkish cheap-eats venues, and the razzle-dazzle and forty-foot whirling windmill of the Moulin Rouge, with its naughty promise of the French cancan.

"Have a look at the size of the doormen outside," I said to my young strolling partner as he checked out the displays, full of exotic promise. "They're a clue to what goes on inside... These are places to run up a bill quickly." A first look at the wild side of life. Even in these furious, neo-Puritan times, Paris remains eternally sensual.

A publisher friend had insisted before we left, "Whatever else you do, make sure before you leave, to have one big night out in Paris. Really shoot the lights out!"

Such excellent advice! For days we checked menus, looking for the right spot. It turned up close to home, a little bistro with a menu as fine as we saw anywhere. For our gastronomic repast, we arrived direct from La Tour Eiffel and had the lot—a perfect *prix fixe* dinner: fresh sea bream, rabbit in mustard cream, raw goat cheese salads, a chilled Beaujolais, thick custardy desserts, and coffee—oh, and cokes for the kids. Ask in French, and the waiter won't be nearly as snooty. A marvellous repast well worth applauding, and we did, to appreciative bows from the staff. Like Dr. John sings, "Such a night..." Indeed, for our sharing of this as family, we were truly grateful.

A friend like Justine is a double blessing. With an elegant old house in the country, she keeps a *pied à terre* studio in town. After transiting from Brussels, we surface on the Rue d'Hôpital with the Seine behind us and the Jardin des Plantes on the right. As ever, the 5th arrondisement feels right. Lugging our gear, we pass small restaurants on the French boulevard of lead-roofed apartments and proceed through a corbelled passageway with our wheeled bags clattering along the cobblestones. Inside, we glance at a traditional-style courtyard, stone walls four stories high, polite curtains, pots of geraniums in wrought-iron racks outside kitchen windows, a bicycle leaning against a wall; tidy, well-kept.

Willowy as ever, Justine steps out to greet us. She asks if we've managed to avoid the jams on the road; farmers are protesting, making the drive impassable.

"We're okay," we assure her, stepping inside for tea and a catch-up conversation. After a chance to settle in our bags and have a wash, Justine, eager to get on with the day, asks if we might start by calling into Nôtre-Dame. What better way to begin? We set off together and savour the river views along the walk. The cathedral is a short walk up the embankment along the Seine, and unfailingly, it's a wonder inside. The enormous vertical walls, the dim light, the *vitro*—its inexpressibly blue windows—and its piety are an overpowering experience. Yet there is something else about this holy place: as Justine notes simply, "It's *France*. For me, it's essential to my life, this feeling I get of being in touch with something important, bigger."

We breathe in the cathedral's subdued fragrance, redolent of myrrh, and stand in awe before the magisterial windows. Lighting a candle, I observe Justine genuflect and cross herself beside Kwan-shik. In a world of art and teaching that has grown spiritually sterile in North America, perhaps throughout the modern world, I can't think of another artist friend with this devotional awareness—and here, in Paris especially, this home of art as a form of political engagement.

Refreshed, in warm sunny weather, we embark for the Pompidou Centre, the Beaubourg, as Parisians call it. Today, Justine says, we can view the big summer show.

"What is it?"

"L'Art du Sacré," Justine explains. "It's a big look at how modern artists have worked with this subject." Here is another eyebrow-raising example of Paris and its ability to ride cultural contradictions, to go against the flow of what New York critics consider *de rigueur. Toujours Paris, toujours.*

We wade through some filmy Casper David Friedrich and German romanticism, proceed around a wall, then *bam,* a long vertical image appears that is unmistakably Matisse. Our catalogue refers it as a late sketch from his designs for the Chapel of the Rosary at Vence, near Nice. Something of all this coalesces, and we stand together before the painting and talk about Matisse. "The impressionists were laughed at by the bourgeois," Justine observes. "So in their art, they started to return this disregard toward society—in French we say it's the method of *épater les bourgeois.* It was a shock."

"It means 'Outraging the *boobsoisie,* the comfortable class,'" I explain for Kwan-shik, borrowing the zany term from H.L. Mencken.

"Yes, there was intentional art like that," Justine continues. "Now we have the *shock*," she says, "but not the *art*." Passersby listen in as Justine speaks in her accented English. She guides us on to pair of French artists from the 1950s that she says are worth attention. Jean Degottex, incites our interest; Justine likes him, arguing that "his work *Mono-no-Aware* is a big calligraphic meditation on transience, from Zen." Then we study Alfred Manessier. "He works with *vitro*," Justine says, "with the sense of spirit you get from looking at the stained glass windows in a church."

In a room themed "The Doors of Perception," I enter like Alice in the Looking Glass. Immediately we come upon a series of black-and-white photographs by Allen Ginsberg of Burroughs and Kerouac, and a display of their books in French and English editions. Early film clips of the Beats run in a sequence. Amazed, I move onward and wait for the others to arrive, while admiring two framed images by Brion Gysin, hauntingly simple and beautiful. Gysin created Chinese-style inked ideograms, which he studied as a military translator during the war, and blends in black Arabic-style calligraphic script, which he also studied during his long years of ups and downs in Morocco. The result, on ochre and golden backgrounds, creates an ecclesiastical state of primordial hieroglyphic bliss—atmospheric, like a kind of modern Flemish art—bringing his flowing images up close to the viewer. Kandinsky meets Wang Wei. In a sobering moment, I view the letters of six or seven older writers of my acquaintance on display. "History is descending on you," remarks Justine.

Our first morning in the 5th. Rising early I walk out to exercise silently in the Jardins des Plantes. In the shade beneath a few broad plane trees, I move the *Chi* slowly and watch early morning joggers trot past. In Paris even the runners have style in the way they comport themselves. No one is overdoing things. There's a McDonald's across the garden; I sneak in for a quiet half-hour and drink strong coffee.

By mid-morning we are driving south into the countryside. The Île-de-France region surrounding Paris contains about twenty percent of the French population, although the physical size of this landlocked administrative area comprises a fraction of the national geography. Twenty-one townships lie within the department of Essonne, where we are headed; our friend's family has established roots here. The road is busy, passing through numerous small communities, and we have an opportunity to observe the shifting demographic mix outside of Paris, noting the young and their fashions, which are not much different than any other global metropolis.

We arrive in the town that serves as the centre for Justine and her country neighbours, its little streets linked around a small public plaza with the municipal library and town hall. Adjacent is a series of *bar-tabacs*, and long residential streets punctuated with shops, bakeries, clothing and shoe shops, *fromageries* with windows that invite you to a world of cheese inside, and Greek donair shop fronts. Japanese, Lebanese, and Vietnamese restaurants run from the centre to the railway station.

Justine's family territory is leafy countryside dotted with stone farmhouses. We arrive at her home, and it's a picture-book image out of *The Three Musketeers*—a squire's home built of limestone, with steep roofs, storm shutters, interesting architectural bends and wows in the rooflines; the whole place is held together by rustic wooden beams. The gateway into its large courtyard would have been sufficient for a coach and horses; there is a vestigial falconry, granary, outbuildings, and a high stone wall enclosure around the hectare of property. Beneath a wispy sky, the spreading apple tree outside the open kitchen door is a paradise cloud of blossoms this year, and along the property walls, a hedge of stinging nettles.

Chickens cluck and peck about the grass throughout the day, scratching near the kitchen door for scraps, and beyond the wall a shady, lazy river courses through woodlands flanked with deciduous hardwood foliage. Birdlife thrives in the woods and is varied and melodious with finches, redstarts, and warblers. Stepping inside the house, we enter a large, airy parlour with a huge old fireplace. Stained glass windows, huge ceilings, and everywhere the old hand-sawed oak beams, set with mortice-and-tenon joinery, each beam dowelled into place. The oldest portion, the falconry, is hundreds of years old. "Possibly a Knights Templar dwelling at one time," Justine says. "The Templars were active in this area."

The late morning is calm and warm. Seeing Justine is back, neighbours drop by, bring local news. There's a bottle of vin rouge at the end of the kitchen near an open door to the yard and a cheerful gentleman enjoys a glass beneath the apple tree: "The old fellow across the road who everyone appreciates, it looks bad for him the doctors say. Cancer. Ah well..."

Beside the narrow rural road fronted by walls like our own, the lilacs are in bloom, and the fields glow yellow in the sun with canola flowers. It's like a painting by Van Gogh. There's a ruin, bona fide Templar, a healthy walk over the fields, set in an overgrown copse; the limestone corners of the building still show the original chisel marks. The copse is choked with nettles and alive with mosquitoes, so any visits must be quick. I flash on childhood stories—the Crusaders, chivalry, knights in armour, Joan of Arc, the Children's Crusade.

Lunch is set in the shade and sun beneath the apple tree. Artichokes—a specialty from Brittany—steamed with olive oil and *moutarde* dip, red cabbage and sliced apple salad, roast chicken and gravy, quinoa salad, a half-bottle of St. Emilion. Then coffee, and a choice of custard *flans*. Justine has insisted on cooking, and our meal unwinds leisurely. No one tires of talk about food and wine in France, nor of snacking on crusty hearth bread. Always several loaves sit out beside the wine on the sideboard near the door. "It's important all day long," Kwan-shik reminds me quietly. "They fought a revolution for it, right?"

The Artist's Way

With fatigue from our journeys catching up to us, we doze in deckchairs in the sun while Justine disappears in her studio building, working as ever. The country French, we've discovered, labour to their own rhythm, starting early in the day and carrying on through until late afternoon near dinnertime. Mornings and afternoons are punctuated with breaks for a chat with neighbours passing by, a glass of wine, or for coffee and a little time in the sun.

At three o'clock, we walk up a trail and that leads past the woods to a sprawling flat plateau above the village, cultivated from horizon to horizon with canary yellow rapeseed, canola—exquisite to the eye, but a mono-crop for making cooking oil—industrial agriculture. The air is brisk, and there's a stir across the open spaces. We might be in a corner of Saskatchewan. In North America we forget that other contenders produce oilseeds and grain like us. France is top five in the wheat-producing world.

Crunching through the last of the trail, we continue along a quiet road past more walled farmhouses set in remarkably stony soil—large hillocks of raked limestone shards dot the cultivated landscape, the same fill used in constructing the local walls we see everywhere. The soil appears incredibly fertile but is pocked with lumps of stone. We're standing in what was primordial seabed, now more than one hundred miles from the coast. Justine tells us, as a girl playing in the area, she'd find ancient seashells and ammonites to polish and pierce for making necklaces.

"The Beauce, where we're walking, is the breadbasket of Paris, its wheat-growing heart," she informs us, waving her hand across the line of fields. "It's important for two reasons. Food, certainly. Also, the kings could keep their *mistresses* at a chateau in this area. For us it's an hour into Paris by the car; and for them it was maybe a half-day by coach to come here to see their girlfriends for a few nights. Not too bad, if you imagine..."

The broad-minded French. "We've seen those movies with the fancy wigs and beauty marks, sure," Kwan-shik says, grinning. In minutes, several roe deer break from gleaning the fields; we catch their reddish antelope forms moving in the open. It's a restful early evening, easy on the heart here in the Beauce. Across the fields, church spires soar above small villages in the distance like an impressionist work by Pisarro, that underestimated master of atmosphere and landscape. We carry on back home, following a circle route, passing through a stone quarry surrounded by white birch trees full of light.

In the morning, we amble along the river. It's drizzly today, and the trees are young and green. The pathway leads past allotment gardens heavily productive with vegetable plots, flowers, and fresh herbs. "Some of the shacks on these properties might also be where people are living *temporarily*," Justine comments without judgment.

"Homesteads, we'd call them. These are your back-to-the-landers from Paris," I suggest.

Near the end of the allotments stands a house that Justine says is notorious for its encroachments into adjacent public lands. As we walk on, a posse of noisy teenagers on trail bikes roars past, slams over a tiny footbridge, and jags across the land-grabber's territory without the least trace of respect. "A modern version of the peasant *jacquerie*?" I ask. We can hear them in the distance, revving through the bush and irritating the grabby owner.

Nearing Justine's we make ourselves useful and gather up armloads of firewood from a covered stack she keeps in the forest. The bush is damp, and tromping back and forth by the river's edge, I discover that my left shoe is leaking in water. *Merde.* It happens on the road, bumping about in the same footwear every day. I still have my good shoes handy that I save for working appointments and hope for the best.

Justine has made nettle soup from the garden for lunch, a favourite here. The stinging nettles grow high: "It's getting to be a tradition when you arrive," she says. Then after a change of footwear, we're off into town to see her new exhibition at the town hall. I've written something for her brochure, and we've had it translated. In the large exhibition rooms, we contemplate our friend's paintings, big images. In some she has incorporated traces of family documents she began using in a series of works begun after a trip we made with her to Vimy at the Somme. Her new work breathes with vivid colours and a Taoist sense of flow and movement. It's another blessing.

We roam the damp streets of the town, and it's reassuring; no need to go far, we're just here, where we want to be. But, unaccountably, my good shoes are leaking too. "Is this a sign?" I ask the universe. *Breathe deep.* Since we're in town, we call in for excellent charcuterie at the butcher's. There's no rush; everyone has time for *bonjour*, it's expected, really. The old ways. And while replenishing our dwindling bread supply with three loaves at Justine's favourite place, the staff recall us from our visit a year earlier and present Kwan-shik with a cloth bag specially for carrying baguettes. *Merci!* There's some cheeky talk among the women about the shape of the bread and how well it works with brie or camembert, the soft cheeses, a source of mirth among the merry wives of France. We depart and I walk head erect, maintaining dignity, toward the municipal library on the Rue Sainte Croix. Maintaining dignity is *très, très important* in la belle France. You learn this from watching Inspector Clouseau.

At dinner a neighbour from across the way joins us, Claude. Following the courtesies of French introductions, we speak in English. *Bon.* During our last visit here, we'd crossed to his grounds for a look at his Celtic *menhir* stone, a massive upright archaeological marvel the size of a Volkswagen. "It was a boundary marker between two tribes before Julius Caesar arrived," Claude records modestly. "The Senones were settled in this area and the Parisi to the north, where the city is today." Over a glass or two of vintage Bordeaux from Justine's old cellar, the conversation is eclectic, swirling around the history and origins of the stone.

"Do you know Asterix the Gaul?" Claude asks, referring to the French cartoon hero who regularly wreaks havoc and revenge on Caesar and the Romans. "The stone is like that, *Gaul.* We may have forgiven the Romans, but we haven't forgotten their names or where they lived."

Justine's latest country-house dinner is memorable. On the heavy oak mantel, three opened bottles have appeared—a Chateau Pibian, a 1990 Pauillac, and a Lynch-Bages Grand Cru. "Yikes, get a look at those three numbers," I whisper to Kwan-shik. "It's starting to look *serieuse.*" Claude politely handles sommelier duties; the French fall into their roles comfortably. Justine peeks from the kitchen and suggests we might want to build a fire for a little later; at last, something I can manage. At her table, the dishes arrive: a platter of sliced sausage and *boudin,* blood pudding with apple sauce; her main is a potage that has taken ages to simmer, of pureed squash and vegetables, home-style, served on artisan-made flowered soup bowls and plates. Then five types of cheese with baskets of this afternoon's bread. The conversation flows in two languages, and we do our best to surf the wave, our tongues lubricated by the superb wine. Around us the heavy limestone walls measure three feet thick, plastered around massive timber frames. Tudoresque, but inescapably French with their apricot pastel emulsion and the enormous country fireplace, no hearth to speak of, with Justine's pair of large hounds close by.

We talk and talk, there is so much to say—the recent tragedy at Nôtre-

Dame with its glorious roof crashed and burned; the disillusionment of the young with institutional faith and governance; the *gilets jaune* protesters in the streets every weekend and how it is populism in another guise. Now it's the *casseurs*, the die-hard types who keep it going. The damage they have done in Paris is scandalous. But there are no conclusions to these topics, we agree. Tonight, isn't it more auspicious to talk about art?

A retired public commissioner, Claude has his own opinions. "For a lot of the people involved, contemporary art is about business," he concludes. "Naturally, I am very glad that Justine's work receives recognition. I like very much what she paints. But the modern, well…"

Justine looks on equitably. "In international art, a lot of the shows are provocative, aggressive. For me, art should raise the spirit of people."

"Let's not dismiss all the moderns—Justine is modern, right?" Kwan-shik interjects. "What about Andy Warhol? He's someone who gets your attention without being offensive. I mean, he's a bit crazy sometimes—soup cans, Marilyn Monroe, Elvis. He makes it look easy, and he stopped all the snobbery by making ordinary stuff popular."

Justine shifts, looking like she's about to disagree, but then lifts her glass of wine. "You are right, he changed the position of the artist, like Leonardo," she proposes. "That's important." Ah, we are in agreement that we all like Andy Warhol, even if his work isn't always so interesting. Tonight we are in France, and we just like Andy. Justine has a crafty spark in her eyes: "He changed it like Robin Hood."

The following day we move slowly. It's a low-stress opportunity to spend time with Justine in her studio, examining her recent work and hearing of her new experiment with "land-art," more precisely a floating mandala concept using threaded corks recycled from occasions like last night's. "Sometimes painting is about not having things, your materials, completely under control," she asserts quietly. "With my new project for a floating exhibition, the water talks to me. There's the colour, the surface of the pond; it's a discussion like Monet with his water gardens at Giverney."

"Do you think that you can truly 'teach' people art? Or do we have to discover it individually?" Kwan-shik asks.

Justine thinks a moment, and confidently emphasizes, "You can learn how to cultivate 'sight,' to draw, to sculpt. What you *can't* learn is what has to be inside you—the *motivation.* There are a lot of ways to arrive at keeping the voices inside us alive. It's important to find your own discipline. For myself, I must work every day. Working alone means you must always confront the self, so you must find your own self-discipline. So, I'd say it's not so much 'Can you learn art' as 'Find your own voice.'"

Chartres Cathedral is magnificent, probably higher, more dramatic than Nôtre-Dame de Paris. It is built on the site of an ancient grove sacred to the Gauls and their druids. After the defeat of Vercingetorix, the great leader of the Arverni, the victorious Romans cut down the trees and installed a Roman temple in its place. This in turn was pulled down and rebuilt as a cathedral, and a deep ancient well from Druid times still exists beneath the altar's north pillar. Justine recommends we make an expedition this day to see the cathedral.

Drawing nearer through the farmlands, we pass by hedgerows and weaving fields where young wheatlets are taking shape, next sunflowers, and then water towers and wind turbines set on low ridges against wild lilac and three shades of green. From ten miles off, we began to see the famous spires.

It's hard to walk up the suddenly steep hill on which the cathedral precinct is situated and not think of the Druids, of the holy grove that's still buried beneath the sprawl of towers, buttresses, enormous stone arches, and soaring spires. A truly medieval cluster of constructions.

Inside the cathedral, past astounding stone work—hand-chiselled almost a thousand years ago—the vaulting is stupendous. How was it done? The space has all manner of optical features and the most phenomenal stained glass. The effect is truly psychedelic. It's all one can do to sit in sheer awe.

It's a huge inner space. In the centre, restoration work cleaning the ancient stones is an ongoing campaign—everything slowly being returned to what it must have originally looked like—clean, brilliant with light and stained glass colour. Overpowering. People are at prayer everywhere. In a chapel, you kneel and witness the *Sancta Camisa*, purportedly the Madonna's holy cloth wrap for her infant, Jesus. With a thousand years of pilgrimages to this site, countless numbers of the faithful have been drawn to its reverential presence.

The cathedral interior does grow chilly, and we exit for a small lunch nearby. Le Pichet is tiny, located in the downstairs of an antique shop. A billboard outside advertises its thick potage. It's delicious. What captivates, however, is a seafood salad dish as delectable as it is unusual:

> Seafood Salade Cocktail
> Smoked fish, grapefruit, raw sea-scallops,
> scallions, crayfish, lemon, fish eggs, on lettuce
> and watercress. Light vinaigrette.

What a treat! Good bread, homemade watercress soup, delicious coffee, and an affordable tariff. While we eat, we swap thoughts—living with more awareness, more kindness, more stillness, and about not surrendering. "Enjoying small victories is critical in this way of life," Justine comments about her role and work as an artist in France. "Even if I feel sad, art is still a meditation for me. I can ask myself, what is this sadness in my drawing?"

She's preparing for her next show, the land-art undertaking in Brittany. "It's a discussion. Emotions and materials go together. And the more you're in touch with the deep inside, the more you're in touch with the world. Like the men who worked on the cathedral a thousand years ago. Their work was an expression of their faith."

At the Somme

Two years prior to visiting Chartres, Justine and a friend drove us three hours north to the Somme Valley where we wished to pay respects at the battlefields where my grandfather fought in WWI and was badly wounded. We'd travelled while the day was young and bright, stopping at highway turnoffs where, in France, you're likely to find a top-quality Paul's bakery-restaurant serving meals. We aimed first for the Canadian war memorial at Vimy, just outside Arras, then wandered back toward the area of Albert, an hour south of Lille. The battlefield heartland. The Somme is a pretty river, not too wide, and the country there pleases the eye. You can practically smell the wild thyme growing in the field hedgerows. The Vimy Memorial is unforgettably tragic, beyond words, as if Michelangelo had sculpted it for Canadians. The sculptor/architect Walter Allward designed and completed it after fifteen years of work, calling his monumental work a "sermon against the futility of war." It's a holy pilgrimage site for Canadians and Newfoundlanders who fought on this ground with a horrific loss of life. Few attend here without tears.

Enormous flags greet on the way in. A long winding walk leads up to the memorial. Sheep graze the meadows, as much of it is still, a hundred years later, out-of-bounds for walkers due to the danger of unexploded ordnance. The path leads through a wood and stunning moon-sized bomb craters have been left in place, grown over with grass. The size of them is scarcely imaginable: survival would have been impossible. After the hamlet of Vimy, a stiff slope leads miles off to Lens with its huge coal pits; after a long view, Arras lies in the distance. It was an October Sunday, which in France means that the shooting season has begun, and the French are avid hunters. Ironically, here at Vimy where so much carnage unfurled, in the hedgerows and thickets at the foot of the first long slope, hunters were firing bird rifles and steady cracks reverberated through the chilly afternoon. All about the countryside, pulled over by the roadsides, groups of men in bright jackets gathered or dispersed with their guns and bag for the day.

No one has dry eyes at the Vimy Memorial. The gigantic scale of its twin towers and grieving majesty are unforgettable. The gravity of endless rolls of names chiselled on the marble walls is sobering beyond calculation. We are in France, but it feels like Canada, a Canada weeping for its fallen men. On that raw, blustery day, the wind swept across the sloping fields the way that machine guns must have raked the advancing Canadians from the heights during the savage three-day attack in April 1917. You spend hours here, breathing the spirit of the terrible wartime sacrifice made by young soldiers not much older than our children.

Driving south from Vimy toward Amiens, we passed through the Bapaume-Albert area where so many shed their blood. My grandfather's regiment fought brutally at Courcelette village along this road, but no one seemed to recognize the village name any longer. Then driving past a nameless country hamlet, I spotted an old name marker fallen and half buried in the grass. *"Arret!"* We pulled over and looked about. A nondescript village of a dozen or twenty well-worn houses, with a small church; beside the road stands a memorial to the Canadians buried nearby. I asked in French, and Justine backed up my inquiries, but of several locals we spoke with, none seemed to know or care much about World War I. Perhaps a look at my grandfather's army service photo that I'd brought for just such this occasion? *Non*, monsieur. A place of prayer *seulement.*

Before leaving for this journey, I'd studied the army's campaign reports of the battle. From the memorial, I glanced backward to where the Allied lines had been; Allies to the left, Germans to the right. The reports describe house-to-house fighting, men with bayonets, machine guns. The British over-ran the German trenches and held them for only a few days before a counter-attack drove them back. This was a typical back-and-forth story of that nightmarish saga we know as the Battle of the Somme. In four months of unspeakable human agony and chaos, the Allies lost half a million men and gained five miles of ground. The Germans lost as many or more. At Courcelette, it was the Canadians who later cleaned up.

That night at our hotel across from the train station in Amiens, I came down with a raging fever that became severe bronchitis I wouldn't shake for weeks. Amiens, where Joan of Arc led her army against the English invaders, has another of Europe's splendid cathedrals from the 1100s. So much history all around one, layered with brilliance, art, old religion, wars, the lot. Justine noted the historic synchronicity of the numerous cathedrals commenced within the same eighty-year period, and that could each have taken literally hundreds of years to complete. Standing in the surprisingly small square in front of the cathedral, it took little to imagine my grandfather descending from the troop train at the railhead that had made Amiens so valuable in the war. "He'd have seen this monument to civilization on the way to the killing trenches, or on a short leave from the front," I reckoned. My grandfather, Maurice Cross, wasn't the only soldier here. More than a million soldiers would be killed along the Somme Front, 20,000 on the first day alone. The badly wounded numbered three times that.

Back in Paris, the hourglass is running out on our latest visit. Justine asks if we would like to see anything else. "*Oui*, we'd like to visit Edith Piaf's gravesite in Père Lachaise." We train to the cemetery in the 20th arrondisement and meander amongst the tumuli and cluttered rows of sepulchres and huge stones. "Look... Balzac." Not far away is the graffiti-pocked monument for Oscar Wilde by Jacob Epstein. From there, past the memorials to Parisian Jews who perished under the Nazis, we arrive at Piaf's simple, well-maintained resting place. What is there to say? Like the little sparrow of Paris, we don't regret anything at all. Not too much, anyway. Beside us, an older woman weeps by herself. Modigliani is close by. Then after a few minutes turning and edging past stones, we pause for a mandatory look at Jim Morrison's roped-off memorial; did he finally find some peace here in Paris? It's still early, but already a crowd of young internationals flocks to see him. A female gendarme keeps quiet watch nearby.

To the Place de la Nation for coffee and a last extravagant dessert in the warm weather—an *Île Flottante* of puffy meringues and chilled custard—then on to one of the city's best little-known attractions, the Rue Daumesnil with its elevated Promenade Plantée, known as the "rooftop of Paris." You can stroll four kilometres atop an old railway aqueduct lined with potted shrubs, trees, and flowers. "You need a friend to show you some things," Kwan-shik says, amused: "This is awesome—I hope the neighbours don't mind us looking in their windows." We're thirty feet in the air and, only a short stretch away, the kitchens, bedrooms, and madames of the 12th district watering their perennial geraniums are eye level with us. Nobody takes any notice. Along the Viaduc des Arts section, there's an art show on exhibit, "Art en Balade," and the district's arts council has organized the exhibition *en plein air*; it's a maximum-fun walking tour through the city's overlooked eastside. With our walker's fatigue, we're ready to sit down in a tidy green square named for Charles Péguy, *mort à la Somme.*

"Another public square named in honour of a poet," I comment. And though I don't remember much of his work, Péguy has left us one eternally apt quote—"Everything begins in mystery and ends in politics."

It is five in the afternoon, and we are in the unfashionable 12th, but this means nothing to us. The architecture is fine, and we enjoy the cool of the hour at another café terrace where we assess French art, and some Taoist and Buddhist parallels. Motor scooters whine past, squealing around the tight bends into alleyways. Young people began drawing near on the sidewalk, listening in, offering questions—"*Excusez-moi*, is it Zen you are talking about? Do you know *existentialisme?*"

"Couldn't be more ideal, could it?" Kwan-shik asks Justine, laughing. "Talking Zen and philosophy in Paris? All they need are a few berets."

Walking back to Justine's, we stop at an ATM. A side street next to us on the corner is empty, yet no sooner do I withdraw my cash than a playful young dude, lean, fast, African, approaches and with irritating handwork up near our faces and a fast patter begins whooping it around us with a *futbol,* dancing, blocking our path. "It's fun, isn't it," he calls in French patter, dribbling with tricky footwork, his arms and hands beginning to touch us up and push a little, coming on too strong and way too close on a quiet street. A professional. Instinctively we feel for our wallets. The trickster street-thief is grinning, all teeth and laughing, and I focus the deadeye on him, refusing the distractions of his arms, wary of where his tripping foot might come from. He dances in close again, the Artful Dodger, dribbling with his fancy footwork and another touch. I smile myself, moving three firm finger points to his solar plexus and a short flex of wrist, full of suggestion, clearing him off *rapidement.*

"Va te faire foutre!" Justine snaps. The F-bomb. We carry on through narrower streets in dimming light, more alert now, toward the Seine and the Pont d'Austerlitz across the river.

With time for a last afternoon together in the Latin Quarter, we pause for coffee at a zinc bar we know on the right bank near the Église de la Madeleine. Concerts are performed here in the church amid its collection of sculptures and dome mural of heaven commissioned by Emperor Napolean. *Wait!*—up near the saints, isn't that figure, uh, Napolean? Apparently he made it through the pearly gates regardless.

The night before, after entering Paris, we'd eaten bowls of Japanese noodles in a place not far from the Place Saint-Michel, then strolled back to the studio in the dark. It was lovely along the Seine; students were enjoying music and dancing, and with the warm evening, the banks were awash with young lovers and elderly couples, everyone sitting on the various lawns nearby or along the stone edge of the quays. Talking, drinking wine from the bottle; hundreds upon hundreds of happy people made merry from Nôtre-Dame eastward. With darkness, musicians arrived—African drums, brass horns, guitars, and fiddles.

Every hundred yards or so, a natural little amphitheatre is built into the river promenade, and people flock to sit on the steps; when the musicians begin, they filter out to dance—the Tango group, the Swing dance group, the medieval folk group; all organically self-defining; no one pushes or is unruly; no police presence of any note. The populace tidies up after itself. Justine says it's been like this in Paris since she was a girl.

"Just consider," I said, "an anarchically self-governing citizenry taking summer pleasure along the river... If this had existed as a possibility, or was allowed in North America, would we have needed the upheavals of the sixties?"

"You had the hippie times in San Francisco, wearing flowers in your hair, didn't you?" Justine asks. "Here, we had student riots in '68, like a revolution. It was happening where we are standing, all around the 5th, close to the Sorbonne…"

We continued along the Seine as the last booksellers closed up their stalls above the river. For old times' sake, we paid a sentimental visit to a café for a nightcap. This is the way Paris is supposed to be. As she prepared to return to the country, we took leave of our friend with laughter, fun, pictures, wine, a little sadness. *Au revoir, au revoir!*

The world is better on the road. Lebanese, Filipinos, Georgians, Portuguese, fellow Canucks, Kiwis, Venezuelans; we don't meet many bad actors. Perhaps we're getting older, but there's a fellowship one shares along the Camino of life, like in Chaucer's tales.

Our last morning: As always it begins with a glance from the studio at the long view across the rooftops toward Sacré-Coeur, emerging into view from its grand shadow with the sunrise of the coming day. We tone up on coffee, fruit, and leftovers from the night before and set off calmly, towing our cases through the great front doors beneath a grey sky in dry weather. Passing a public dustbin on the street that is always clean in the early hours, I bung in my useless leaky shoes. Holes in everything; pilgrim shoes tattered as a sieve.

With a final wave, we pass the waiter at Café de Raphaele, and he waves back. Together, we clatter down the street toward the metro at Austerlitz.

2002-2019

THE PARADISE VARIATIONS

I'd been training with my old Tai Chi master, Sifu Ng, for three years when Kwan-shik and I rented a shack by the bay in an isolated hamlet on the island of Maui, replete with lush jungle and orchids at the door. Heralded by an unimaginable chatter of songbirds, dawn comes early in the backcountry, with the sun rising east from the sea. From this humid morning air, guttural WAHOOOOS, shatter the primeval heaviness. Each day, I rose quietly with the birds and went fishing for our dinner.

One morning, as usual, I made my way up the lane to an unused jetty. The hour was calm, the nearby sugar mill abandoned. Across the bay, coco palms swayed in the breeze. Patiently, I cast out my line, trying baits without much success. Content for the while to let the line dangle, I surveyed my surroundings. The breeze was young, and the waves rolled in nicely without any great force. Not a soul stirred ashore. *Magic.*

With this perfect tropical occasion to move with the Tai Chi, I paced off my space on the old wartime dock. Breathing steadily, deeply, I commenced moving. Growing sure of my footing, I progressed through the movements, sweeping to the right and Grasping the Bird's Tail. Rocking softly in reverse, and stepping lightly to the left, I caught a glimpse of the land and sea. Shallow whispers blew in from the bay; then something unfamiliar began. From the open ocean, I sensed my old master rise before me like a presence.

Breathing, I felt his spirit enter and move through my limbs. I let his presence flow of itself, and as I moved, my posture and expression attuned themselves with a softness and fullness I had never previously known. The chi was moving, I knew; more palpably than anything I'd experienced before—a steady magnetic pulse through my limbs and torso. I understood in that moment it was Sifu who directed its course. I moved about the jetty, and he showed me the way: the ripple of his fingers unfolding in space; the weightless sinking of his sweeps and feints; the inward turning of a heel; or the effortless thrust of a knife-edge hand.

What I had seen with my eyes for the past three years was transpiring within my own being with only this sense of occurrence. No thinking; none at all, for the merest intimation might dissolve the visit spontaneously. Only movement, being present, full attentiveness. Breathing as the body wished.

"Don't think," Sifu taught. "Only move." No-Mindedness as the way to mindfulness, I heard him saying.

The changes progressed: Raise Hands Up, Slap the Face, White Stork Spreads His Wings. I sensed the old man very clearly, his visage blank of expression, moving like a frond in the wind. No resistance.

The litany of Yang forms and mudras worked on, transforming and completing itself as a course. Late in the second set, I became aware that I was flying solo again, although Sifu had been there; that I knew. I played through to completion, rooted in fullness and harmony with the Tao. As I concluded—Carry Tiger Back to Mountain—there was emptiness: Perfect Tao. Immanent. Holy. All One.

My life altered in Hawaii, there by the sea, but I did not dwell on it. The heron dance, I knew, had changed, transformed by a wholeness beyond physical form or self. Clearly, something had coursed through my limbs, and like those struck by lightning, an indefinable cognizance has remained ever since.

"Though I do not know its name," Lao-tzu says, "for lack of a better word, I call it *Tao*."

2002

THE RIVER TO TIR NA NÓG

IRELAND

"The land of happy wars and sad love songs"

—Richard Sheridan

At a certain point, I realized that I had to take my son and daughter to Ireland. Raised on the Pacific Coast, they needed to know in a deeper way who we were and where we came from originally. This proved one of the wiser things I've done as a dad; Kwan-shik was with us every step of the way. They call these "roots journeys" for a reason. Oddly, after nearly twenty years exploring and working throughout Asia, this process of introducing my wife and kids to our family "back in the old country," I also began reconnecting in a truer way to myself. It's a dilemma peculiar to immigrants. Since then, I've been returning regularly, digging a deeper well of acquaintance and memory.

In Ireland it's about the land. Every scrap has been fought and refought over for the past five thousand years. That's the textbook version. What it's really about is the heart. In the north-central counties, we've been cattle people. That's what the land says to you in Irish Gaelic where we come from—*eallach*, "cattle." You can read about it in the *Táin Bó Cúailnge*. This story of the Cattle Raid of Cooley predates Black Bart and the cattle rustlers of the American West by a thousand years, and that's only the written account. The oral stories take us further back, "way back" as Van Morrison sings. A powerful queen, heroic warriors and strong maidens, a great red bull, poets, love and hanky-panky, and a spot of envy and thievery: the histories they report go back to the dawn of who we are as the Irish.

Ours isn't a renowned or noble family clan; we've no golden monarchs or reincarnated 12th century lamas or wizards the way they do in California. But we have one notable: our national composer. Ireland's version of a travelling delta bluesman, Turlough O'Carolan the Blind Harper. Before Jim Morrison and Mick Jagger, he was the man with the tunes. When he wasn't off laughing with Jonathan Swift, he was an itinerant bard, led by a stick-boy, travelling big house to big house, swapping his company and music for a bunk and a meal. When he died, they drank hot milk and whiskey from his skull, a cure for the epilepsy. Otherwise, we've looked after cows or laid bricks for a living. Somehow I slipped through the net and got an education, so I can only blame myself for the result.

On the upside, as my father used to say, "It's only a sin if you take pleasure in it." Then he'd drain his pint with that peculiar smile the Irish know as "the dark pleasure," and we'd have another.

Dublin airport's not so big, and it's easy to arrange a lift. The restaurant is hearty and fresh, and you can buy smoked kippers from Howth, or a loaf of soda bread to take home with you. My cousins Emer and Shivon are full of news and questions. On the way to the farm, we stop in Monasterboice for a pub feed where the first draught of Guinness is good. Then we're back on the land, a long hour by motorway north of Dublin, thirty miles east of Cavan town, above a lovely sweeping glen. We have graves to see, then staying up late, drinking tea with a nip, talking and talking, kids running around, and neighbours finding reasons to pop in from over the way.

Nicky, Emer's husband, is forever outside, working at something or romping with the baby, Ellen. The three young girls are red-haired and giggly. Celeste, the eldest, is a fine Irish dancer. On Saturday we drive into the North for a *Feis,* a competition where she excels. My first time in the North, and all the old Trouble times fears are there, but we're in

Armagh, St. Patrick's stronghold, at last. It's a heart-warming time, scores of children river dancing and jigging. We leave with invitations to call on all sorts of people next time.

We walk into the Daybreak shop down the road next morning; it's bright and tidy. Micky at the till says, "You're back again, are you?" Two years since he last laid eyes on us. Grand memory here. "And how are things in the wilds of Canada?"

It's always wonderful in Cavan. My first morning I walked over to say hello to old Uncle Terry. We're in the cowshed and me still dressed tidy-like in travelling clothes; already I'm recruited to chase after a cow that's as big as a runaway truck, "Into the feeding pen! On the double now!" There's no sharp sense of occasion in the country, just jobs to be done. It's like being in heaven to be home in Ireland.

Cousin Emer, making dinner, says, "The more and more children you have, the less you're meant to worry."

At eighty-nine and still fit enough to work the cattle, Uncle Terry in his tweed jacket and flat cap, is the poster boy for rural Ireland. Old beige trousers, pale blue pullover, thick madras shirt, long underdrawers. He's stiff and chesty, bent a little, walks with his blackthorn stick—exactly like your postcard Paddy grandads. I gaze in silence at the patches of weather-burn on his cheekbones and temples. The language is simple here. No media interpretation necessary:

"Oh, by Jayzus the weather is fierce, so it is."

"Christ, don't you know..."

"Is the weather turning fair then?"

Recurrent conversation, with everyone everywhere all the time, about the weather and the silage. Swapping reports: "There's showers ahead; men are cutting the fields over the hill, in Monaghan, across in West Cavan..."

With his wife in heaven these past twelve years, I've never heard him say an unkind word of any living soul. Who else can I possibly say that of? We sit by the glow of a low coal fire, his cheeks warm and coloured—no modern furnace will do that. Can we add a little peat for the flavour, the scene? "On a long winter's night, it's a safe man!" says old Terry.

On the Monday, we walk up and down Shercock, the closest village of my father's youth. Sunny and cheerful today, with its one main street of brick and whitewashed stone homes. We take out coffee and soda bread, walking up to St. Patrick's at the edge of town. In the churchyard, we study the plots and memorials. The Carolans are here.

The church has rectangular seating these days, with the altar erected in the middle of the congregation and pews lined up beside it in parallel rows. The stained glass windows are still superb—of Mary, Jesus, and Joseph. Beside the altar, offertory candles are always lit for your family to the Queen of Heaven, the ancient Goddess, suit yourself. *Ave Ave*... Throughout the Catholic world, we call on the ancestors, light candles in their memory, remind them that we're thinking of them down here and could use their blessing and protection. Outside, the precious graves, tended with great care.

"Say what you like about the Irish," Father Ollie says, "but they know how to look after their dead."

"Yes, no... maybe."

There is no definite word for "Yes" or "No" in Irish Gaelic, for the verb "to have," nor for the possessive pronoun "mine." In Ireland this same ambiguity about language transposes into English. Uncle Terry doesn't say No. Instead he provides a litany of reasons why something is not a good idea. Glenys, my sister, says our dad would never give her a straight answer either. She'd ask if she could go out on a Friday night. He'd dawdle and stall: "Let me think about it," "I'll get back to you about that," "Maybe... " It drove us crazy waiting for a decision, she says.

"He was *considering*," Uncle Terry explains.

About the possessive business, in Irish you can't say "This land is mine." In Irish one says "I belong to this land." Father Ollie, who spent time in the missions in Africa, says it is very like this in Nigeria too.

"Isn't it a hard world?" Uncle Terry says, on hearing a weather forecast calling for more summer showers, the hay still not cut. I glance at him near the fire. He's smiling as he makes his complaint, just another way of passing the time.

"I'll Be Off Now—but First a Story..."

"Always look on the bright side. We've forty shades of green here." Kathleen, Nicky's mother, winks, unflappable. She's down from Blaney, ready for off on the bus with her friend in the morning, for Letterkenny in Donegal, then on for the shopping in Derry. But first a story.

She tells us the tale of an English friend that came over on holiday. Helen had lost her father and was grieving, so Simon, her husband, a nice fella, brought her to Ireland where her dad was from. This one evening they walked into a pub out west in Galway. They were enjoying a drink when a man walked past, an older fellow. Helen looked up, followed him with her eyes.

"He looks like my dad," she said.

They studied the man as carefully as they could without drawing attention. Shortly, Helen walked up to the bar and, taking her time, ordered drinks again, using the opportunity to look at the man who resembled her father.

"It could be him," she said to her husband when she returned with the drinks.

The husband had a look when he went to the toilet: "You're right. He's his walking double."

He sat alone, keeping his own company. At last, Helen said, "I'm going to speak to him, introduce myself..."

Helen approached the man and brought up his strong resemblance to her dad. As it goes, he told her he was from Portugal. It seemed odd, well out of the way from Ireland, but strangely enough Helen's father always said that his family had Portuguese blood in them, some distant relation, or the Spanish Armada. Helen's husband joined the two, and they enjoyed amiable conversation through the evening. They talked about how pleasing they found Ireland, especially the West. The gentleman said he found it pleasing too; it was why he'd settled there. "The sun seems to shine more warmly here." He smiled.

The hours passed on. It was time to leave. Helen asked if they might have their picture taken. No problem at all. They took a number of photos, and someone snapped a picture of all three together. Such a lovely evening; they all left beaming.

Helen had her holiday photos developed back in England. She wanted to see the pictures from Galway first, with the man who looked like her father, to show them around at her work. The snaps were soon ready. She went straight to the Galway portion; there was the famous Spanish Gate, Eyre Square. She saw the picture of Rabbitt's Pub with its sign and knew the images of the man who was her father's mysterious double came next.

"And?"

There was nobody in them. No one beside her, or her husband. No one at all, other than them. As if your man had never entered Rabbitt's that night, or they'd spoken with him, seen him with their own eyes. Talked with him over an evening's conversation.

"Sometimes it happens like that in the West, in the Gaeltacht," Kathleen avers. "There's no explaining such things. God bless all here!"

With the rains and damp, the silage is no good this year, Uncle Terry says. Some farms are cutting and baling it the same day, not drying it out. If the silage is too damp though, it moulds and gives animals the cough. Hay is drier, about twenty percent moisture. Animals feed on silage during the indoor season when they're penned, November to early April; generally, they prefer the more moist silage. "An acre will give ya twenty-seven and a half bales of silage," Uncle says. "This will leave enough to sell. But poor weather this year and still five more fields to cut…"

Then another fine dinner; pots after pots of coffee and tea. The table conversation is all about the neighbours, the young people coming up, the olden days, the cost of things. I'm struck by the return to olden names from Irish for the children—Emer, Oisin, Shivon, Ruari, Finbar, Aoife, Sean.

"In the old days, it was a sign of being backward."

"Aye, but now it's a sign of education. Money will do that," Colleen says, from the house at the turn in the road.

People don't have numbers on their house in the countryside. The postman knows each place by a name, a location. It was like this in the original census documents that I purchased copies of from the county government. Unchanged in a century, thank God for that. Then it's another long evening talking with Uncle Terry and Shivon, the younger cousin who looks after him. It's the old custom for the youngest to look after the parents. Marrying late was the Irish country custom; or sometimes not at all. Every country family has bachelor uncles, unmarried aunts. Nicky, Emer's husband, has a Cavan brogue so strong you can slide on it; rough and ready with a big heart and no putting on airs. A fierce family man. That's their style.

Friday lunch at the Slieve Russell Hotel in Ballyconnell. It's large, beautifully designed, a country club with fabulous grounds, more like a grand home, surrounded by fountains, golf links, and gardens. In one enclosed garden, we see a sign announcing the Aughrim Stone. There's a light rain, but we find it easily enough, a great rectangular stone, cut with one narrow width on the angle. Excavated while the hotel was being constructed and resited nearby, the 4,000-year-old cairn stone has marked an important grave. Uncle Terry stands beside the ancient stone: "Gawd knows, it's an auld 'un," he grins and coughs. "Four thousand years old?"

"Nearly as old as you, Uncle Terry..."

It is also the centenary of the Battle of the Somme in WWI. Our host, Father Ollie, suggests reading Tom Kettle's poem from Dublin, "To My Daughter Betty, the Gift of God." Kettle was a nationalist activist, a crusading journalist who fought for the poor, and a friend of the Easter Rising rebels, 1916. Also, James Joyce's dearest friend. Kettle's wife, Mary Sheehy, was Joyce's early muse, and he bases Miss Ivers on her in "The Dead."

Cousin Joe from my boyhood days calls over. He'd got wheels and we're off, trucking about the countryside. We drive to Bawnboy and Jampaling Tibetan Buddhist Centre there. "A bit of Himalayan Vajrayana in the auld sod," I cod him. We're greeted warmly and treated to a tea and biscuits interview with the old Lama who teaches there. And what a wonder, we've had an old friend in common, the late Lama Bakula, an Indian appointed ambassador to Mongolia. *Om Mane Padme Hum!*

Next, on to Cootehill, where we drive Uncle Terry to get his hearing aid checked. It's your one-and-a-half-street Irish town, but filled with every small shop you might need. The lassies Celeste and Marie tell us their Granny bought her bread in a shop here forever, and that we can buy some lunch, so we do. At Niall O'Leary's deli, there's a table and four chairs. "Cavan goat cheese and the best blackcurrant jam in the world," Cousin Joe says, a soulful American blues track percolating from the back. Marie, the younger sister shows off a bit, writing in the guest book in excellent Irish.

Everything changes. Nowadays you've to eat it all standing up, but it wouldn't feel right to get to Ireland and not *buail isteach*, or drop by here.

It's wonderful to be in the deep countryside—extraordinary beauty and stillness. My father's presence is all around us. And there's Seamus Heaney's reminder about the dropping away of our sense of "creeping privilege" in his *From the Republic of Conscience*. Constant reminders we're in the holy Isle of Ireland.

Next day we stop in Kells for a bowl of soup, delicious potato and leek, with a look at the round tower that stood against the Vikings here in County Meath. *That* Kells, yes, historic home of *The Book of Kells*, the celebrated illuminated manuscript. Fair play to the Arabs with their calligraphy and illuminations that run right alongside. Near a pair of ancient cottages behind the tower, Joe drags me to an elderly lady he knows. She'd shown him in last time. The cottages are associated with the olden days, and their monastic stone cells are where Irish scribes kept Europe's learning alive during the Dark Ages. As Thomas Cahill argues, didn't the Irish save civilization?

Returning home, we talk by the stove where Terry sits keeping warm. "Would youz like to see the cattle?" he asks, raising his head. "All forty head?" Agreed. He leads us out to the deep loam of the fields, setting off downhill with his herding stick, still spry. He is gone a long time. Finally, the cows snort up the hill, and we find ourselves surrounded, noting the young Limousin bull, a ring through his nose, who seems docile enough. I think of Ulster's affinity with cattle, with the raiding in the *Táin* that gave Yeats and his circle their insight into the myth tales. And there's Yeats himself, borrowing images from this same countryside and people, "Down, down the glen/ rode the bold Fenian men…"

Out of Dublin and past Drogheda, then thru Slane where the pop stars are all marrying in the castle these tax-conscious days, we head for Newgrange, the 3000 BC Stone Age court tomb and astronomical observatory. It's capably organized—a low-impact visitor center with a good café. We're in the Valley of the Boyne where so much political trouble began, where King Billy the Dutchman defeated poor bewildered James I, but not without hauling the faithful Irish into his woes. There are still hard feelings, but we're keen for the Stone Age instead. Awesome vibes inside the long tunnel, pitch dark with only the one magic light source. We are among the world's oldest traceable human constructions—massive burial chambers created from huge stones then covered with earth, like walking into the centre of a pyramid chamber, only older. Ireland's the boss, eh? *Whew.* Andy Warhol should have made it here. You stand in a stone chamber that's lasted 5,000 or more years; the King Kong-sized entrance pillars feature mystical, spiral patterns hand-chiselled before the age of the diamond drill. It's as pagan as Paddy McGinty's goat and has never collapsed yet.

The Magic Thrush

In July, up and off early for Sligo in the West Country, Cousin Nicky driving, his step-dancing daughters in the back. The weather isn't much, but we're on the road after a feed of breakfast, heading out narrow country roads for Enniskillen and a short switch through the North. We pass through Belturbet, then Belcoo. Hand-painted signs out front of farm homes along the road proclaim the new Orthodoxy: Tourism, Farming, Health, Fracking. The contamination concerns are the same in North

America and everywhere the energy corporations are searching for deep gas reserves. Then a fortified police barracks as we cross into the North, a postcard image of the old imperial grab. Nearby in the republic, thatched cottages. The landscape shifts, drumlins giving way to flatter land in Fermanagh and then Leitrim.

At Glenfarne, a sign on a shop wall where we stop for a break remembers Sean McDiarmid, a rebel leader in the 1916 Rising, born near here at Kiltyclogher, and one of sixteen executed at Kilmainham jail in Dublin. Their deaths set off a rage that grew to the ferocious independence struggle under the bold leadership of Michael Collins. They raised heroes in specks on the map like this.

We pass the green bens of the Dartrey Mountains with their round peaks, nearing Yeats country. The land appears noticeably more like the West—Connemara. Rock-faced cliffs, mist above treed slopes, sheep grazing. On our right, Glencar Waterfall and Lake, on the way to Sligo. We near the town and ahead, unmistakable, is Ben Bulben, the table rock. Grey skies, rustling elms. We turn into the churchyard at Drumcliffe, St. Columba's, Church of Ireland, where Yeats's family were rectors of the parish. They're honoured with a plaque.

From a tree in the churchyard, a thrush flies straight to my arm and leads me to the poet's grave. We stand and read Yeats's epigraph as he wished. The thrush does not leave; the girls are a little awed. Then it rides on my shoulder for an hour or more. We wander about the churchyard, and it's clear the poet is in the bird. "We'll call him Yeats," calls the young one: "a poet to a poet." We read Yeats's inscription again and walk over to the teashop. The girls bring out coffee, and people join us for a photo; they've heard the story. The Irish understand these sorts of things. Again, the bird does not fly off. Lines of Yeats come to mind, and I recite a handful them for the youngsters—from "The Lake Isle of Innisfree," "The Song of the Wandering Aengus," "Crazy Jane," "When You Are Old."

It's a hard moment, looking on the poet's stark grave. You'd think it might be adorned with flowers. But no, just the blue-grey stone face, upright. His epitaph from "Under Ben Bulben":

Cast a cold Eye
On Life, on Death.
Horseman, pass by.
W.B. YEATS
June 13th 1865
January 28th 1939

Yeats rides my arm to the gate where we must leave. I wonder what will happen. Only then does the bird fly off and return to its tree, finally, with our many goodbyes. The poet's lines from "Wandering Aengus" that Judy Collins and Dave Van Ronk sang:

The silver apples of the moon
The golden apples of the sun.

When I walked into the wee kitchen, Uncle Terry asked if I'd fancy a drop. "Here? I thought you were a Pioneer and never touch the drink," I replied, baffled. Like many who'd seen others ruined by liquor, he took the religious pledge in his youth and stuck to it.

"Not at all," he tells me matter-of-factly, pouring a dram into the coffee Shivon has made, then a nice dollop in his tea. "I've never touched a drop in my life. I only keep a small bottle for the medicine. It's the doctor's orders. For my chest and to stop the coughing. And maybe a small one to help me sleep."

Shivon gave me the look: *Don't say a dicky-bird.* "Ah, well I can see that, Uncle Terry. My mother and father did the same, with a little hot water in the winter. It clears the passages."

"So it does!"

Another of life's mysteries in Ireland, here in the tidy little house with the roses outside and the cows content in the field. We just surf the wave.

"Will you have another?" he asks, a little louder this now, with a touch of colour in his cheeks. Any minute now we should be back talking about Cavan's immortal 1933 All-Ireland football victory. "Aye, I think I'll join you in a small one, Uncle Terry. There's a nip in the air tonight, do you feel it?"

"So there is..."

"As my father, God rest him, always said—" Old Terry's watching me now, nodding. Does he know I'm only pulling his leg? "Isn't it only a sin if you take pleasure in it?"

There's the nod again as he pours gently. And the sly wink.

The Holy Mountain

With the weather breaking, but never certain to stay fair, we head as a family to Croagh Patrick, the most sacred mountain on this holiest island. Croagh Patrick is the spot from where St. Patrick drove the snakes out of Ireland, after fasting forty days and nights during Lent, and being tormented by the demons of the air atop the mountain place so remote that even the thought of a scrap of dried kipper would draw screeching crows and jays like a magnet. The trail looks simple enough; peasants here have trodden it barefoot in penance from before the time of the Celtic saints. We found out why soon enough as the lift and scrabbly ground left us first puffing, then stopping altogether to catch breath as we moved higher. During our summer solstice day climb in June, we saw perhaps a dozen other pilgrims—but at the end of every July, an official day of pilgrimage draws thousands.

At one thousand feet, we took a break with the cooling air: three degrees Fahrenheit for every thousand of altitude, I recalled from school days. The wind whipped up, and we put on our jackets. Before us the huge bay of Clew spread with its smatter of small islands; we were at sufficient elevation to see the green and blue patterns of water depth in the sunlight. Below the trail, rough stony grass supported loose flocks of sheep that cropped away at the falling slopes.

After forty-five minutes, we made a ridge that promised a respite. Tramping horizontally a short while, we caught our breath and approached the second pilgrim's shrine for circumambulation and prayers before returning to the wicked inclines of the upper slopes. The loose scree looks impossible to scale. How people walk barefoot over the jagged flints for hours is inexplicable. From the ridge, we saw a scarf of cloud building steadily around the peak, and passing the ruins of old hermit huts, we tackled the last third of the mountain, the trail reminding me of China.

For the last half-hour onward, Croagh Patrick is a dangerous agony climb. The elevation is steeper than forty-five degrees, an astonishing incline, slippery underfoot, and a test of faith and nerves as rain spattered the higher slope. I grew concerned for Kwan-shik and our children and checked back for any sign of faltering will, but they pushed on with me even as light dimmed in the lowering cloud. Our feet slipped and chipped and pecked their way up the rocks.

From time to time, the sight of a ruined hut on a small clearing recalled the sanctity of our enterprise, dispelling the fear of the moment. Might it have been different on a balmy summer's day with crowds around us? No doubt. We ploughed upward with the winds and rain sprays sweeping irregularly all around—the demons of the air that St. Patrick met and conquered.

The last ten minutes were filled with trepidation. What had seemed a last long vertical ascent fell off apparently to another stiff, plodding climb, and with no clear sign of the top, we worried about our descent down the dodgy steepness and poor footings. Then two young Americans, man and wife, surged down the trail from above. "You're nearly done," they called. "We're making tracks because of the weather..."

Another five minutes and we were there.

A small stone chapel known as the Oratory secures the top. Scattered about the flattish landing are ruined stone huts, and in a corner, a pile of empty plastic bottles. A third shrine of pilgrimage exists for circle-walking and recitations of prayers, and toward the eastern edge of the summit, the ruins of a pre-Christian ring-fort wall. This was the historic clan territory of the O'Malleys. An image rose in mind of Ronnie Drew, gravel-throated frontman of the Dubliners, singing "Oro Sé Do Bheatha 'Bhaile"—"O You're Welcome Home"—in Gaelic after the historic Irish run at World Cup Football glory in 2002. Ever since, this homage to the great Pirate Chieftain Grainne O'Malley, and to her undying fame, is sung at hoolies all over the country.

Atop the mount, a solitary figure knelt in prayer before disappearing from sight, another pilgrim, not dancing on the mountain as I'd joked to friends, but kneeling to pray and honour the Divine as has been done here since time immemorial. We offered our own gestures of thanks in the mist, high above the sea which we knew lay somewhere below. It was remarkably still, and we were Irish, very deep, from way, way back. Transcendently being family here. Then for a precious moment, light and a warming, a lifting, and the sea of cloud below and around us was illumined with a soft golden glow that we bathed in. With the long sparkling view of the sun sinking in the west, just as quickly it shifted gray again. We knew enough to begin scrambling down, our walking sticks picking the way, authentically in a state of grace together, before full darkness settled.

Into the Mystic, in Connemara

Out of Westport, we made our way to a friend's house at Errislannen near the Connemara shore beyond the small town of Clifden. The house sits on the edge of the Atlantic looking at clear water straight through to Newfoundland. Ivan is a naturopathic physician and does good work; he hails us in with a wave of his arm toward the Atlantic a spit away. His family have had the house for decades. Just a few days after the solstice, the evenings last brightly until well after ten PM, and even at midnight and one AM, light glimmers on the horizon. This is the Ireland you see on postcards: small lime-white cottages on rocky land, stone walls everywhere to clear up the fields, and the crazy-looking Connemara sheep that roam at will—shaggy horned zanies with blue and red dye marks to identify them to owners—blue heads, red arsed, dots and circles.

Errislannen is as good as it gets. A remarkable guide, Ivan introduces us to an old Gaelic gasser, the village postmaster, and I acquire some of the language on the spot, or more exactly at the end of a small dock; is this what Otis Redding understood—the song of the Soul? I think so. "Watching the tide roll away..."

From there we knock about for the next five or six days: local bays and beaches; crossing the burren to Roundstone; drinking Guinness in the pubs where you bring your kids along too, my son facing up to his first drafts of stout; music; and step dancing. Local lamb, fresh stone-crab claws. With night falling, we ramble about the boglands, and Ivan takes us into a haunted ruin: great spooky stuff!

Guinness and a little whiskey drinking help keep out the chill. We've passed turf bog cuttings on the way, and it's still the heating source of choice. In Clifden, there's good music from old-timers and young buskers alike. A lot of Europe longs to be here. A couple of evenings each week, there's a trad night in the local town hall. They're a rootsy event, ideal *craic*, or joviality, for the visitor: musicians and guitars, singer and accordions, all the old tunes. You'll see a lass dancing fine step-work, or a white-haired gent telling a hoary old tale. Toward the end, it gets Gaelic, and the national anthem, "The Soldier's Song," is sung in Irish, very heartfelt. It's like Cape Breton, on the wild Atlantic Coast, 4,500 miles away in Canada.

Connemara's is a bleak coastline; the weather rolls in from the sea and turns frowsy. Ivan looks out the window. He's bought a double-masted yacht and sailed from Norway to Connemara, following the route of the old Vikings. Next year he sails up to Reykjavik, following the route of St. Brendan. Before Columbus, before the Vikings, Brendan the Navigator sailed with his monks and pet heron on his bow straight across to Newfoundland, where they blazed the trails the Vikings would follow.

Up the coast from Errislannen, the ferry to Inishboffin Island, home of the lamented old singer and fiddler Dessie O'Hallaron, leaves from Cleggan. Again, another good pub where I dry my wet socks and shoes by the fire. Our daughter is riding horseback in the rain on the sands of Omey Island a little to the south—crossing at low tide like Mont Saint-Michel in France. We follow the line of surf-riders out of sight, and Ivan drives us, five minutes by car to Cleggan. Up from the shore, we set off walking over fields. Rain whips up again; the ground is swampy, but Ivan looks about and finds what he wanted, calling us over. In the corner of a broad field walled by stones with a long sweep of pasture behind us, a stone dolmen tomb stands monumentally thick and strong as it has for thousands of years. Two lengthwise slabs of stone capped with a mighty block, forming a rough tunnel of uncountable tons of rock.

"Someone must have really liked the place," Ivan says of the ancients.

Back at Omey, the island has a holy well and a ruined church, circa 7th or 8th century, and the nearby Little Hill of Women. Days later, we return from Ivan's place in a storm, and he roams the country barefoot like Heathcliff out of *Wuthering Heights*. We're an hour and a half from the Aran Islands to the south—they're visible on clear days from a high ridge above. Offshore is a further litter of islands and reefs. Beside the tiny ruined church, set in a hollow to deceive marauding Vikings, old graves are scattered, bones dug up by rabbits that litter the area. It's a passionate place, wild. We roam about, and my son Patrick and I build an altar amid the ruins; why else would the sea gods cast up the shoulder bone of a bottlenose dolphin on the shore? The holy well, *an tobhair fechin*, was blessed by St. Fechin, who with St. Patrick and St. Colum converted the Irish to Christianity in these parts. Newborns were dipped in the well for protection against chest fevers. We stand in the powerful summer storm and drink in its power, our heritage, and not a little of our faith.

The actor Peter O'Toole liked it here, Ivan says.

Our last evening, we walked with Ivan and his dog up the road, around the shoreline by a fishing cove. We'd slashed a tire on jagged rock driving in there our first night. Nearing the small crossroads up from the house, we were set to turn back the quarter mile, when I glimpsed a mysterious stranger, *an fear beag*, out the corner of my eye. There seemed only to be the floating head and shoulders of him above a dry stack wall, in a flat cap, brown clothes, moving away from us toward boggy land behind a low drumlin. A lean, rugged islander. He glanced my way, the look on his face sharp, far from welcoming, somewhat chilling. It's a mystery, difficult to put out of mind. The others had walked on. All of us passed him. No one else said they'd seen him. Next day, unaccountably, the family record I'd been gathering disappeared entirely. It's forever another world in time here, near the very edge of things temporal and eternal.

Three months since my last visit, a call rings through in the dead of night: Uncle Terry has passed on. We scramble for a ticket over to the funeral. Old Terry died quietly in his sleep.

It's an epic scramble to get over on short notice, via London, then double back and catch the bus up from Dublin to Shercock. Straight away I'm taken by the old customs, like a film. An open coffin in the house, all the neighbours coming in to pay respects. There'll be an early funeral. Priests and prayers: suddenly it's ancient Ireland again. I'm asked to speak for the family. "You're wearing your father's shoes now, lad," says Eamonn Corlis from down the road.

I stand beside the coffin during prayers, and the floor starts to wobble. I've been in the air fourteen hours, and it feels like I'm aboard ship. I haven't slept and it's strange. Cousin Joe comes walking in the door. A happy reunion in solemn times. Oddly, while we're sad, not everyone is morose; people are busy getting ready, being helpful; everyone has a role or a task, and there's plenty of quiet laughter and codding. Like the movie *Waking Ned Devine*.

The funeral follows a night of prayers in the house, the ritual in progress as I arrive. Deep in the country, coffin in the small room, mourners coming from all around the valleys to sit with the family in consolation, all solemn then stories and laughter, prayers and priests. All offer cedar blessings and water in unbroken rituals that go back to Druid times; holy water and prayers I haven't heard in long years; passing around photographs, reciting old stories about the deceased, remembering, remembering in whispers, then laughter, more tears, crying children—the whole tapestry.

In the morning, an old bell tolls over the fields, and hundreds of mourners gather along the lane to the farm, self-organizing, all farmers, like 18th century. Afterwards, a long line of cars snakes slowly along the narrow winding road to the graveyard, past people lined up at lane-ends. Then a last slow drive through the small town he knew best, arriving at the country church where my father walked to mass as a boy, and carrying the casket on our shoulders and again later to the burial site; water blessings, incense blessings, throngs of people saying the decades of the rosary in the open air; children crying; deeply pious. I've never seen anything like it outside of Indian and Tibetan towns in the Himalayas, or maybe Italy, like a film by Francis Ford Coppola. Haunting and beautiful. Death brings everyone together, all Celts, red-haired, rows of earrings, long hair, tattoos, flat caps, old worn faces from working the land in the ancient, ancient ways. Thank heaven they haven't been obliterated by modern times. Uncle Terry is having me welcomed back into the tribe, to who I am.

Funeral rituals go on for three days in the country and are not that different from when Synge wrote about Gaelic Ireland. Carrying the casket over fair distance to the burial place, the *Ave Maria,* blessings in English, in Gaelic, all from another time; hundreds of mourners passing after the service to offer sympathy, everyone greeted, thanked by the family.

"He was a hard worker"—the highest compliment that can be paid by these neighbours whose lives are a long working day, every day. "A grand worker he was…" over and over, God love us.

The men of the family lower the coffin, then as the flowers are laid down, take shovels and fill in the ground behind the church. Father Addie from Nigeria says the last prayers. People call by the house for days, and there are visits ourselves, back to the priests, thank-you dinners. The involvements give families plenty to do, and they forget their grief for a moment or two longer. In the country, people have plenty of time. Oddly, given all the stories, never a drop of drink in sight.

When Kwan-shik joined me soon after and we hit the road once more, I knew that we were nearing the river of Tir Na Nóg in a polite one-street town where the signs were in Irish and the colours of the pubs and houses were purple and gold. It is not far from Cavan, but the land is gentler. Some of the fields were looked after less and were filling in with gorse. Radio Telefis Eireann na Gaelige featured announcers with softer voices, mostly women. The music shifted too, from hurting American country songs to ceilidh tunes and folksy songs with a twangy, keening edge. The houses we passed flew the green and gold.

Uncle Terry once chuckled, saying, "Sure, when God made time, he made plenty of it." His voice doesn't leave us now, but the conversations grow more one-sided. Holy Ireland. This beloved land of saints and sinners. Truly, as Sappho declares, "What cannot be said, will be wept."

2006-2017

DANCE YOUR PRAYERS

BRITISH COLUMBIA

This summer I've been dancing, tribal dancing especially: long night juking to pagan rhythms—mega-heavy African crisscross drumming, Aussie didgeridoos, Celtic abandonment dance, magick vibrations. Real musicians, real music.

At a rainforest communal gathering in the Pacific Coast Range, I experienced a new generation of grail-questers. Up-and-comers from the Burning Man scene, their group is defining a new space in the culture for themselves. Taking as trail markers ideas like sustainable development, permaculture, and living lightly on the land, they're optimistic, green, educated, diverse. We'll call them the Rainbow People. In a world begging attention, they're happy to stay out of the limelight.

In the sunnier days of the late 1960s, we called it Peace and Love—airing, pairing, and sharing life's simpler riches. Now, Rainbows just say "Dance your prayers." I like the sound of that. The public expression of joy and meaning is alive, dissenting, and well, a kick up the pants to the tyranny and oppression of the Patriot Act crowd. So I was glad to join in as these latest generational rebels shaped their own rhythm and dance.

We were in a remote mountain forest you can't find without a secret decoder ring. Invited to lead a workshop for the wilderness event's free school program, I swapped stories with participants who had journeyed into the bush from Vancouver and around B.C., and from across the prairies, the U.S., and three or four nations overseas. Quickly and efficiently with battery-powered hand tools, they erected a communal kitchen and dining area, ringed campfire areas with stones, and jerry-rigged basic, functional composter porta-potties. Young gardeners, carpenters, architects, publishers, web designers, students, and artists told me of a desire for a community of their own fashioning. Raised with the material comforts of modern consumer culture, like my own lucky generation in the sixties, they share an appetite for transcendence that mainstream culture doesn't much offer them—a sense of community, of place, of the sacred, of something to *belong* to. Not simply *more of.*

They used no put-downs in their conversation; no one bad-mouthed anyone because of this or that. The feeling in the air stayed gentle, like a bowl of Okanagan peaches. Where in the sixties we were suspect of money, Rainbows are smarter. They understand its importance. They've reflected on how to improve things for their own time. What they disdain is greed.

As a cheerful survivor of late-Beat scene hipness, sundry psychedelic whoops from the sixties, and proto-punkoid slams at the Smiling Buddha in the late seventies, one thing charmed me in a benign kind of way. Rainbows have a belief that the socially transformative enterprise they engage in is a genuine historic first. Amen, I say, recalling how this very belief sustained me on a 1,000-mile solo hitchhike to Haight-Ashbury fifty years or so back at the age of seventeen. What larks and bumps that brought back to recollection. With this in mind—and having recognized one or two of the wolfish types near the edge of the campfire as the drums and guitars got down on some heavy first-night rhythms and the tribals got dancing in the forest of the night—in my remarks to the group I worked with next day, I alluded to how sixties activism also attracted the usual opportunists inevitably drawn to the banners of Liberation and Freedom. *Younger brothers and sisters, Be mindful.*

I shared the idea, too, that tribal dancing is part of a perennial generational impulse reaching back traceably as far as Stonehenge. And that while each manifestation is new, simultaneously it is also a seed-spore of what's gone before.

Thirty years ago, tribal cultch in Vancouver was Wreck Beach, an early-eighties nude guerrilla, Buddhist eco-surf, Socialist romanticism.

Before that, punkoid nihilism and trashy fashion. Ditto the vacuous pap of seventies corporate disco that followed the psychedelic upheaval of sixties Peace and Love metapoetiks. Previously came the Beat optimism of the fifties and before that, Charlie Parker's bebop overdrive outa Kansas City, big band swing, jitterbug craziness, and intoxicant-fuelled mania of Jazz Age Roaring Twenties, not to mention fin-de-siècle Paris of Baudelaire, Verlaine, Rimbaud—Bob Dylan's heroes. Choose your elixir!

And always there has been the dance. Before Rome it was the Dionysian rites in ancient Hellas and Eleusinian priestly Mysteries of Eygpt echoing neolithic, shamanic, Bear Mother whoops of Eurasian/Siberian wild folks, but most of all the ancient stone-loving, pre-Celts with Earth Mother Goddess, Diana, Cybele, Gaia, Green Tara, Our Lady of the Rocks, that's the shrine for me.

The deep forest powwow I observed was about dancing—deeply, wildly, elegantly, with a bonfire casting wavy shapes that dipped and swayed, flowed and undulated—but in the bright intercultural banners and flags that hung and wafted alongside speaker boxes, young bucks had clambered up and roped from trees, and from the conversations and tingling vibes in the air, the unspoken message I picked up was *No fear.* You see this slogan on t-shirts and ball caps, but until the tribal wilderness gathering, I'd really never understood its fuller meaning. With the dancing, it came through clearly: gentle people, young women especially, ethnics, families, and gender-benders just getting along together. No hassles. No one pushing their trip—*belonging* was the trip, without fear of being hit on, or laughed at, catcalled, beaten up, or having to worry about your weight, or hair, or complexion, or your clothes, the way you think, how much cash you're toting, or the way you dance. Just "*you are okay.*"

No fear.

A week later I visited Hollyhock, the beautiful fifty-acre learning and retreat resort on Cortes Island for its twentieth-anniversary bash. The people I met there struck me as matured Rainbows and undoubtedly would have been dancing in the forest thirty years ago, and probably still do if slipped the secret password. I was gratified to recognize how it's still possible to enjoy various points along the educational continuum without contradiction; to be student, participant and teacher within the same week, all within our supernaturally beautiful Pacific Coast Range, and to discover that parts of the world still exist where the spirit of a happy age lives on in spite of the commodification of, well, practically everything nowadays.

Already, September approaches; yet even with the benign warm swimming waters of the Japanese current here, you can feel the first breaths of autumn. The last fat blackberries attract wasps, black-tail deer, and the occasional black bear. I'm still digesting my experience of summer—the enthusiasm, the sometime flakiness and full-time commitment to engaged living that I witness here along the B.C. coast; still measuring it up with other tribal experiences, forging links where I think I've seen them. Thinking is good practice, in moderation. Flakiness by contrast—a wildcard element in old and New Age questing alike—is kinda sugary, but usually well-intentioned, a combination of innocence, new ideas, age, and enthusiasm. It might drive us crazy, but I remind myself that it's gentle and doesn't really hurt anyone—nothing a little mindfulness won't fix. Who hasn't sounded flaky one time or other?

Socrates, that misunderstood bricklaying gadfly from ancient Athens, reckoned the unreflected life isn't worth living. That still sounds right to me. These days, thinking back on the ripe cherries and forest huckleberries we've picked and eaten, the wild crab apples we've sliced and dried for winter, if I'm to choose between listening to the distant howl of timber wolves across the river on a full moon, summer camping night with the drums bomping and thumping and shadowed bodies leaping around the bonfire, or yet another over-priced cultural event in town where the star is too artistically pure to wish the audience good night, it's no contest, I'm for dancing in immortal moonlight.

2016

GROOVING IN THE HIGHER HEIGHTS

NEPAL

Alpine trekking expeditions are the mainstay of Nepal's tourist economy. Few such ruggedly exotic places in the world are as wild, sacramental, and potentially accessible. We were at a café in Kathmandu's Thamel guest house district, owned by an unlikely Swiss proprietor. Small birds flitted in the courtyard shrubs beneath clear skies with thin wisps of high pallid cirrus. After we had been months on Asia's dharma trail, the European coffee and familiar dishes came as an oasis of familiarity.

Kwan-shik learned about Nagarkot from the café owner's Gurung tribal wife. A village speck thirty miles north of town, renowned for its Himalayan vistas, it was an acceptable slog. From Bhaktapur, third principal town of the Kathmandu Valley west of the capital, a country bus grinds upward through the hills to a ridge of a few stone huts and rice terraces. The bus leaves not far from Bhaktapur Durbar Square, or palace square, where its major temple to the deities is gloriously decorated with lively, erotic carving on the wooden roof-combs.

While admiring the wide possibility of physical couplings that can be crafted in wood, we were approached by a local scholar of Sanskrit. "They're unique, are they not?" he inquired.

"Certainly are," we agreed. "Is there a reason why they're here—not that we mind, of course?"

"Of course, of course!" he agreed, introducing himself as Mr. Sharma. "Yes, of course there is a reason. These temples, most of the major temples in Kathmandu area are from the 15th to 17th centuries, built by our kings. Nepalis, you know, are interested in both Hinduism and Buddhism, and these Hindu temples have carvings to frighten the modest gods!"

"Why would they want to do that, Mr. Sharma?"

"Because the Goddess of Lightning and Electrical Storms is a modest goddess of chaste virtue, Sir. And the temple builders not wanting her to strike these huge buildings put the carvings of the lovers here to embarrass her and keep her away! It is quite true!"

We were enjoying our new friend's company. A retired government official, he now devoted himself, he said, to studying books of ancient religious thought. "I studied Sanskrit as a young man—the language of the Vedas; and also Pali, the language of the Buddhist holy books," he confirmed.

"And why have you come on pilgrimage so far from your country, may I ask?" he inquired.

Was it shallow to suggest that the sight of a much lower mountain range along the Canada U.S. border had inspired us?

"We're here to see the old Buddhist heartlands."

Mr. Sharma appeared to consider this. "Then you will be visiting Lumbini near the Indian border, birthplace of the Lord Buddha?"

"We might. We're working our way to Pokhara next. But today and tonight, we're off to Nagarkot to see the mountains. Do you know Nagarkot?"

"Certainly, certainly. But first we should have tea. Will you allow me to treat you as my guests? We will have tea for your journey, and later I will show you to the bus because the roads are too dirty and muddy for you to walk. Please, please..."

We enjoyed the local version of high tea with pleasant Mr. Sharma in the street of the Palace of Fifty-five Windows—a brick structure, dating from the time of the Italian Renaissance, he said, and home of the revered Barking Bell.

"Barking bell?" Kwan-shik asked over sweet, milky *chai.*

"Yes, erected by King Bhupatindra in the 17th century after he dreamed an evil dream. It is a place not liked by dogs."

"Any special reason they don't like it, Mr. Sharma? They've free roam anywhere else in Nepal."

"When the big bell is rung, it sets the dogs barking even today," stated our guide with finality.

Mr. Sharma's rattletrap bus led us upward through rainy, mud-spattered villages, until at a precarious height, we switchbacked into a drier zone. Here, in the middle of nowhere, above an impressive forested gorge sweeping off forever, the bus shuddered to a halt. The driver approached Kwan-shik and led us off. We were bewildered. We saw but one stone hut in the distance. Downtown Nagarkot?

The driver pointed out a trail to the right that cut into the rim of the gorge. Swerving his finger and dotting the air, he indicated bends in the trail. A roof and stone patio came into view down the hillside: an outpost of civilization. Offering our thanks, we set off down the slope. The cottage was an honest little lodge with a couple of rooms near the kitchen. Four thatched stone huts were also set into the leeward side of the hill. We were the sole guests: for two and a half dollars a night we could take any of the one-room shacks. We gave them a look—spartan, dark, musty: we might have been in St. Patrick's Ireland staring at a clutch of monastic stone cells. With night falling, we settled in. A boy knocked on the wooden door selling twigs for the fire. We received him happily and with gestures and pidgin trekker's lingo ordered in dinner.

It was the rashest form of optimism to imagine there might be anything on offer other than the customary Nepali fare of yellow daal, rice, and chapatti. It was thin grub for a night growing bitterly cold. Meanwhile, our chimney smoked pitifully, either by design or from damp fuel.

"Give it up," Kwan-shik recommended gloomily. "I feel guilty about using the wood anyway. We're not helping the deforestation situation much by being here, are we?" Outside, the cosmos was blacker than pitch. We layered ourselves in extra clothes and took to fitful sleep on an unforgiving *charpoy*, or rope cot.

At 5:30 AM we were hiking up the ridge wrapped in head scarves and woollen mitts. The sun had not yet risen. The cold knifed in beneath our shoulder blades. Cresting the ridge which rose sharply out back of our shack, we crossed rough, stony ground and picked our way in pre-dawn light through a double line of animal wire protecting a seedling zone of wiry conifers, fir or spruce.

A jeep track ran atop the ridge, and we followed it through sparse vegetation to a level area that looked out upon a vast descending plain. In the dawn haze, it was an extraordinary vision. We stood upon our vantage point looking directly out to the tallest peaks on Earth, many days' trek across the plain.

"There's a United Nations observation post somewhere up here, they say. Anything heading south from China toward India has to cross this plain. It's the invasion route. A superb observation point," I said.

"Look...," Kwan-shik pointed to the horizon where Langtang, the first grand peak at more than 23,000 feet, backlit with hazy morning fire, began to glow. We huddled together, gazing at the sight, teeth chattering as the sun rose, rays growing in strength, illuminating successive peaks.

One by one they came into view across the horizon: Gauri Shankar, Phurbi Ghyachu, Dorje Lakpa, Ganesh Himal, and Himalchuli, the mightiest peaks on Earth, each from 18,000 to 25,000 feet above sea level. White and gleaming, their pious summits spanned the edge of the world. We hoped for a glimpse of Sagarmatha—Everest—among the cluster of peaks to the east; it was there, but dust from the plain below made positive identification difficult. The mountain peaks hovered midpoint in the distance above a whorl of mist and dust in spectral golden light. Miraculous.

The vista faded quickly. Once the sun had fully risen, dust obscured the easternmost peaks. We were alone above the world with what looked like heaven all around us in the biting chill. For warmth I began the hot, slow dance of the heron and the snake. Kwan-shik came softly across the furze and rubble, and shifting together, one with the other like sun and moon, we played Tai Chi; like Heron and Snake, Happiness and Clouds. Our pilgrimage had reached its apotheosis, the high point of both our lives. We *were*; the mountains *were*. That was all; one, like heron and snake dancing together; eternally, completely present, and the Tai Chi flowed, tingling through our limbs like a Buddha smile between us.

The sentry's arrival was unexpected. A tidy little Gurkha in olive fatigues, rifle slung casually over his shoulder. Friendly, not much English, interested in whatever we were up to. He pointed to a camouflaged tower on a forested escarpment farther along the ridge. Invisible in the dark. The blue banner of the UN fluttered among the trees. "We weren't aware our meditation was under UN observation," we said.

"Buddha Shakyamuni," we indicated with hand gestures, mudras, and the expansive Grasp the Birds Tail movement. It was the best I could do under the circumstances to explain our Taoist practice.

"Like yo-ga," added Kwan-shik for further elucidation.

"Ah, *yoga,*" he comprehended liltingly, his face one big smile. Our delight was absolute. Our head-chopping Gurkha was true-blue, a soul-buddy charmer. Only one thing to do: take photos on the roof of the world.

Our UN chum hugged himself—Yes, very cold, he concurred with a gesture—and pointed to another lodge we'd not seen either, further along the inner rim of Nagarkot Ridge. "*Chai,* tea," he said, motioning with his hands. He walked with us a ways, then returned toward his tower. With a wave he passed through the bush to his post, harking *"Namaskar!"* in farewell, the timeless Himalayan version of *Aloha!*

The previous day's driver had served us more kindly than we realized. Backpackers, he understood, practice a rustic economy. The Tara Gaon Lodge was a hidden peach of a hill resort, but costly—ten times what we'd paid at our stone cottage. We were welcome to sit for an hour or two on the terrace though, where the breakfast *du jour* was hot chocolate and fried potatoes. What could have been better? From the Tara terrace we looked out over the steep wooded valley we'd skirted the day before. A monumental view.

In the distance, we heard the grind of a tourist coach hauling in two dozen or so visitors from Kathmandu. "Looks like they've come for the show," I said, glad we'd been and gone from the ridge.

Twenty-five minutes later, photo opportunity complete, they left, bidding farewell to the mountains with another roar of engines and dust. Calm settled again; birdsong rustled the crisp early air. It looked a fine day ahead, confirming our decision to hike the return leg to Bhaktapur through the splendid valley below. In an hour we were on our way.

With the day merry and bright and the sun at our backs, we headed downhill from our hut. Crossing rice terraces, we descended into a leafy ravine that cut through the forest reserve. The trail was dusty, but the ripple of falling water was never far out of earshot. Occasionally, through apertures in the tree line, we saw small farm holdings; the inhabitants lived in huts much the same as our own of the chilly night previous. Water pots, ploughs, chickens, utility bundles of bamboo poles, and waving children dotted the clearings. They could have been the same remote holdings one passes north in the Yukon toward Alaska.

How do they make a living out here was the logical question. What's it like living on the edge of heaven?

At a junction of trails, a mountain farmer and his son joined us and greeted us warmly in Nepali and with such grace we felt quite special. With hand signs and pidgin lingo, we identified our destination ahead.

The hill man invited us to join them along the trail. Walking in company with the farmer and his son, we quickly forgot any hardships we'd experienced. The land began to sing in our hearts. We said little. We swapped what words mutual intelligence threw out; we smiled and nodded a lot.

The hill man, perhaps five foot five, no more than a hundred and twenty-five pounds, led us with a firm treading gait, even and steady as a billy goat. He wore cotton khaki, a long collarless *kurta* shirt buttoned loosely to the neck over flowing trousers. Over his kurta, he wore the vest seen throughout Nepal made of darker, heavier hempen material with side pockets. The national Gurkha cap sat firmly atop his clipped greying hair, and a tidy military moustache set off his cheekbones and fine tobacco complexion. I'd have said he was fifty; it would have been impolite to ask, yet he was father to the lad. Fifty, I recalled from atlas demographics, was a good long age in Nepal. Did the rigours of hill life age one quickly? The boy meanwhile had taken Kwan-shik's hand and strolled alongside her, pleased as all the world.

"Terrific boost meeting them, eh?" I felt uncommonly well.

"You couldn't plan something like this," Kwan-shik said.

"The mountains, the birds in the trees. It's the happiest I've been for ages." I'd been struggling with one or another of the lingering illnesses that steadily drag you down in the high country. You'd hear of trekkers who set out but didn't return. Such one-way journeys, especially among unprepared climbers, were growing.

For two long hours, we followed the hill man's lead, reflecting on the beauty and transience of this unknown world. Guided by the kindness of these strangers, we passed a fragrant juniper forest; in the manner of the hill man and his boy, we called out "Namaskar!" before each house and encampment. At every holding, the occupants tumbled outside to wave and chatter. The boy sang and swung on Kwan-shik's hand. She sang him a lullaby in Korean. Then the Gurkha sang something like a cowboy's roundup tune, and with only a little pressing, I drummed up "The Wild Mountain Thyme" from my folkie days. We followed a shortcut the hill man knew, and with the mighty transcendental peaks arcing high around us, I shivered at the mystery of it all.

The father and son took their leave of us with happy-sad farewells. He traced us directions in the dirt: we were at 6,800 feet and had to foray across a wide, shallow creek-fall to get to a crisscross of footpaths atop a puzzle of levees. The banked-up levees dissected a collection of narrow *padi* fields compacted within the shouldered confines of a broad ravine, both sides of which were steeply banked and heavily foliated. Tracking the narrow path through the little fields was difficult, but the widening creek signified we'd reached the mouth of a mountain slip and that a kind of alluvial delta lay before us.

Carrying on, with a little perspective, we looked back and could see now that we had reached the first of an ingeniously engineered sequence of small alpine terraces. We studied how the dyke paths intersected and led off to either one side of the valley or the other, and we deduced the makings of a rice-country trail into town. In time, working our way steadily downward, the trail formalized and became a country footpath five or six feet wide. Hot now, not unpleasantly, we left the bushlands behind. Rich fields green with rice and speckled yellow with canola stretched before us. For the next seven miles, we walked through a biblical landscape: women and girls tended fields, water buffalo munched lazily, and at village junctions, old women sluiced down children and cows.

"I guess these folks are the rich farmers," said Kwan-shik, adjusting her pack. We stopped at a junction on the dyke path to beg for water. "They've got villages here; look how many people there are—that's a lot of women working. I wonder where all the men are..." She dug chlorine tablets from her pack and added them to our canteens with a shake.

"They're better off here, you're right about that. The farmers up the mountainside will be lucky coaxing one crop a year from the tiny plots we saw. Compared to this lot down here who've already got one crop on the go, those folks are *poor*."

The hill man and his boy looked different now. Guilt comes often enough on the dharma trail. Kwan-shik had delighted the boy with a gift of foreign coins from her pack. A treasure here, no doubt, we'd concluded. But, staring back at the dry, rough-terraced hills soaring upward in the distance, it might have been wiser to have sent off the father with a few folding notes.

"Maybe," Kwan-shik figured. "Then again, maybe not. They looked pretty happy to me, those people. Anyway, the rains will soon come."

With each mile the road, for such it became, improved. Striding along the raised clay dyke, we saw how extensive networks of irrigation ditches and sluices had been communally arranged. Who owned the land was hard to say; nothing like a big house was in evidence anywhere. Absentee landlords must rule the region, we concluded. The peasants we saw weeding fields or washing clothes and cattle were undoubtedly sharecrop-renters. What that meant for the hill man and his family was troubling to consider. We'd met no more likeable souls in Asia than the heartfelt farmer and his son.

Many creeks and streams such as the one we traversed ran down from the peaks and hills, eventually merging to form the Hanumante River, which flows westward toward Kathmandu. Arriving at last upon a metalled Bailey bridge across one such watercourse, we knew Bhaktapur could not be far away. Sighting the first light industrial buildings on sites that had only recently been padi fields, and with the Parable of the

Mustard Seed and the Tare in mind, we approached the narrow brick alleys of quiet old Bhaktapur town and took our rest.

We settled with munchy samosas and cold drinks to watch the late afternoon drift on. The sun fell lower; men passed by carrying grip bags in hand, often with a chicken poking its head out.

"What day is it?" I asked.

"Saturday, I think."

"Then that's it. That's where the men are."

"How's that?" Kwan-shik asked.

"These fellas passing by are off to Kathmandu. They must work there. Saturday's day-off in Nepal. They've been home to their hamlets and are headed back to town on the evening bus with a chicken from the farm."

"You're a genius…"

Could I argue? We rose together, looking for digs for our next night's kip on the dharma trail. We'd had another breakthrough day on the road. Our hike through the country had things looking our way again. The little hill man wouldn't leave my mind though. As we crossed the cobbled road for Nava Durga Temple, one mantra kept silently repeating itself,

> O Lord of the Three Worlds
> You who surpass even a wish-granting jewel
> Shower him with many blessings.

1985

CHANDERNAGORE

WEST BENGAL

Travel up Grand Trunk Road from Kolkata, and in the heart of jute country, you come upon Chandernagore. A pillar marks the town limits, overgrown in the bush beside an occasionally flowing creek. Notice the pillar in passing, and you will see a faded tricolour upon its facade.

Chandernagore was at one time a French colony, a minor footnote of European imperial history. Periodically, it proved useful to European powers to allow their rivals small appendages to certain colonial territories—dispensations that helped diffuse commercial jealousies, thereby averting hostilities. Mercantile areas like Chandernagore, Madras, and other settlements could also be, and sometimes were, traded in exchange for similar colonial prizes in Africa, North America, or elsewhere.

Chandernagore is situated upon one of the more classic stretches of the river Ganges. Shaped and coloured by dense green jungle and hemp fields, it is above all dominated by the matriarchal rhythms of Mother Ganga, and by a head-swimming humidity that with the scorching sun creates an unreal, purely Eastern languor.

The weekend previous, while traipsing about Dakshineswar temple along the river with our friends, Kwan-shik had met an Italian woman whom she had met before in Europe. Such reunions are not uncommon on the dharma trail and may be predestined. A rest from each other's constant company made sense, and Kwan-shik decided to join her friend

Nola at a coastal beach on a three-day break. The getaway would be good, she said; a bit of time to ourselves, a chance for me to idle with my friends. For the sake of form, I feigned indifference.

"Greedy man," Kwan-shik codded later at Ghuriat Market. "I'll bring you something from the sea. A magic seashell, an emerald, a houri ..."

Uncle Sen picked me up in the firm's Indian-built Ambassador sedan. We stopped on our way to stretch our legs in Chandernagore. Its lingering Gallic presence came as a surprise, more a romantic notion than anything based on hard evidence: "Not a croissant or tabac in sight," I concluded. Only a disused jute mill standing silent and empty by the river, looking for all the world like its industrial cousins, the redundant woollen manufactories of the British Midlands.

For a quarter hour, we shambled about the remnants of what once had been a fief of the grand republic. Not that the architecture suggested anything of the sort; Chandernagore was as much the usual unkempt, dusty road stop as anything else we'd seen of once British, once-French, or modern Indian variety. And yet the raised sandstone tricolour pillar suggested more—the *Liberté, Egalité,* and *Fraternité* of all that is La Belle France. The lance-point grille of the huge work yard gates alone was worth a fortune overseas: they could have easily opened onto the Elysée Palace.

"Rather a bit dead looking, I should say," Uncle Sen mused, scuffing at heaps of ironwork about the mill yard.

"It's so still," I said. "As if time stopped here a hundred years ago—still ready to clink into action. Everything so well preserved..."

The torpid heat and silence of Chandernagore preserved a sense of total vision; as though, in the late morning light refracting from the Ganges River, one was seeing for the first time a place much dreamed of since childhood. The abandoned brick piles of the mill were as emblematic of Balzac or Dickens as of Sanskrit India.

Uncle Sen led the way along a levee bank, and we gazed across the astonishing width of the muddy Ganges. The frantic dust-whirl of Kolkata was far away. This was the agricultural heart of a lush, lazy land with a tincture of lime in the air. Once, the steamers had plied a trade here lugging off sisal and sackcloth to the corners of the Earth. Now, only silence; the yawning river pulling heavily toward her great vulval estuary.

"The French planters went dancing in Calcutta, as we used to call it," Uncle Sen remarked. "Nothing here for them; it's a tiny place really... Nothing like the old Great Eastern, is it?"

We had dined at the Great Eastern Hotel the day before, at that time still a leftover colonial relic downtown, built in the 1840s, not far from the Victoria Memorial, with indifferent food and service. Since then it has undergone a complete makeover. Once it had been of consequence, a tip-top establishment for the better orders. Mr. Sen had introduced me to an acquaintance of his from whom I bought a rare pink polished moonstone. A Delhi businessman we met said it was customary for industry men to use the hotel on business in Kolkata. "We used to bring our own whisky and order up red tandoori chicken—they can still do that," he said. "The girls would knock on your door all night, and you had to drive them away if you wanted to sleep."

What would the memsahibs and demoiselles in from jute country have made of that, I wondered? What was it like when once upon a time the ballrooms shone with Irish crystal, when hosts and guests offered toasts *en français*? When a palm court orchestra struck up quadrilles and followed them with "He's the Man Who Broke the Bank at Monte Carlo"?

A river's edge is made for such idle speculation.

The heat of the sun was in no way diminished by the wash of the Ganges, and my attention focused on its burning intensity. In spite of the humidity, a crystalline dryness parched the mind to a stillness so pure that only heaving silence remained. I looked about at heavy trees and vines, at jute run wild, at the tall mill stack, and a landscape that I saw in reality was two-thirds sky. It was utterly Indian, moving not on time but on timelessness. I glanced at Uncle Sen. He smoked and gazed back without inflection.

Then I heard the drone. A mighty swell from earth and flowing river, from the dust and sun-baked bricks of the mill. It sounded like sitar, but not. I heard the droning of *tamburas*, the deep matriarchal chords of the Great Mother, and I knew it in my heart and gut as the drone of God, of Mother Ganga: the drone of the river, the drone of life, of Ra, the Sun. I heard it for the first time on a levee bank in Chandernagore, an old forgotten colony of France on the banks of the Ganges, and have heard it since only when the world is well, with Tao aligning heaven, Earth, and human soul somewhere beneath the cosmos.

"Shall we move?" asked Uncle Sen. A tidy man, neat of person, he spoke with refined economy. Pressing his cigarette underfoot, he turned and led the way back to the black Ambassador.

We drove on and our route veered off through fields of cane, with the thick sweet smell of sugar on the breeze. Near village settlements, men stripped bare to the waist swung machetes in the sun; others, men with sons, plucked silver fish from throw nets among reed ponds. Enormous munching buffalo were led off by shining herdboys, any of whom could have been young Lord Krishna himself. Everywhere the land was lush; everywhere men and women were intent about their work, smiling readily when observed. Work was the purpose of the day, it seemed, was of the landscape lying east of Chandernagore but, paradoxically, was at one with the broad levees of the jungle's edge.

Mr. Sen drove British-style on the left, and from hanging out the window in the sun, my arm burned scarlet. I pined for shade. Another hour and we arrived at his home.

As soon as courtesy allowed, I went splashing in the Ganges with Uncle Sen's children as my guides. Uncle Sen and his wife Didi stood watching from the shade of a large leafy hardwood. "Do you feel cooler now?" he called.

I laughed. "It is good." Their boy was already diving from my shoulders.

"Then that is as it ought to be!" cried Uncle. "You will remember this, where you were, and how it was!"

If I answered, I cannot recall. The youngsters kept me rousting and jousting, and my feet sank oozily in the muddy bottom.

"Remember when you were here in India," Uncle said. I saw him smile beneath his moustache, a glass of Rose's Lime Cordial in hand. "Remember how it was when you came and bathed with us, with the children. This is the sacred water of our Holy River. You are healing in our Mother Ganga!"

1985

IN POLAND *DZIEN DOBRY* MEANS ALOHA

Poland doesn't always leap to mind as a travel destination. Stuck in a bad neighbourhood between Germany and Russia, normally it has been a place to get away *from*. Historically, its fertile agricultural plains and abundance of natural resources made it a magnet for foreign invaders. The long Cold War period with its Communist bosses only made conditions worse.

As a student, during one summer job filling in graves, I was lucky to have a memorable Polish boss. Mr. Arendarski was a small, impeccably dressed gentleman with a smart moustache. When things were quiet, he'd invite me to his office for coffee and a chat. In this fashion, I learned about Poland's greatest authors, including Joseph Conrad. This unusual boss encouraged me to understand that there was more to Poland than the horrors of Hitler and Stalin during WW II.

Invited to Warsaw and Silesia to present a series of lectures and film viewings, I arrived with Kwan-shik after a lousy transfer through Frankfurt where the airport staff was rude and officious. What happened to the god of German efficiency?

Entering a former Iron Curtain state for the first time in years gave me butterflies. In 1972, I'd arrived at the Hungarian frontier by coach from Vienna to Budapest. Nobody I knew had ever visited the Communist zone, though I'd met several who had risked their lives to escape it. The border brought to mind a bad movie: watchtowers, searchlights, anti-tank barriers, officials with attitude in jackboots and Gestapo peaked caps, carrying machine guns. Before they left the bus, each passenger got an evil-eyed glare, and every last soul said a prayer that he or she wasn't leaving with them. They liked to terrify you and keep you that way until you left the country. Belgrade was less harsh, and I got drunk with North Koreans in Bulgaria. In Rumania I learned black-market currency trading, and in the Soviet Union, they busted me for buying a pretty girl an umbrella. That's my story, and I'm sticking to it. My memories of the Socialist workers paradise hot spots were of a grey, joyless world.

Flash forward. Arrival at Warsaw's Chopin international airport went smoothly, followed by a dreary taxi commute through endless blocks of Socialist-era worker flats. Drab, featureless, the suburbs presented the same numbing character I recalled from the Soviet Bloc days, now referred to as the Period of Stagnation. Meanwhile, our hard-of-hearing driver hummed along to accordion polka favourites blaring on the radio as we passed yet more cheap sectional housing. Architecturally, Marx and Engels have a lot to answer for. What have I gotten us into? I asked myself, sheepishly glancing at Kwan-shik. After thirty years of liberation from the Reds, why was no one updating these places?

Warsaw's vast boulevards and wide buildings set back from the streets are strangely unsettling, yet this is a green city and mothers push baby prams through local parks. Nearer the heart of town you detect a shift—livelier shop fronts, cozy coffee bars, entrances to modern underground metro stations, a sign in English announcing "Chopin Concert Tonight."

At a tight roundabout, we swing into a side street of unexpectedly cramped buildings. From outside, the Hotel Harenda is so unmarked you can walk past without noticing it—ideal Socialist anonymity. "We've landed." A statue of Copernicus, founder of the heliocentric system, sits on a plinth in front of a museum in his honour across from our hotel.

Checking in is easy. Poles are handy with language. Everyone says "*Dobry*—good." Okay, there are no elevators. *Dobry.* You lug your case or pack it up a grand staircase with landings to stop and puff along the way. Corridors are clean, bare of pictures; it's basic and respectable throughout, and for a handy downtown hotel, rates are forty percent cheaper than

North America or Western Europe. You want swank? Try the Hotel Bristol down the road and bring your wallet.

At evening, Warsaw's air is crisp, the streets alive with animated young people walking in pairs and groups. Cafés and restaurant patios buzz with activity. The vibes are homey, bohemian, smack in the centre of the University of Warsaw precinct—"Yes, that's it, straight across the road."

Ambling down the wide tongue-twisting Krakowskie Przedmiescie, a main artery to the city's major points of interest, you pass the Church of St Joseph's the Guardian, a rare historic building that survived WWII. The Presidential Palace with beefy-armed soldiers in security positions is nearby. We see more than a few on patrol, but they're friendly and can provide directions unlike those in Beijing. *Dobry.* A turn on Krolewska Street, and you're at the Tomb of the Unknown Soldier. In size, the vast plaza is along the order of Tiananmen Square. Within it, a single line of Greek-style marble columns are all that remains of a palace destroyed by Germany; at night they are dramatically illuminated. It's a deeply moving memorial, guarded by young soldiers, engraved with the names of battles the Poles have fought through multiple wars. The magnitude of Poland's history hits home. Young lovers stroll past, hand in hand in the dark.

In 1944, after years of Nazi occupation and suffering, the Polish Home Army rose in rebellion. The ferocity of their uprising stunned everyone. The Wehrmacht counter-attacked with Panzer tanks and Stuka dive-bombers. Revenge squads undertook a deliberate destruction of Warsaw that razed eighty-five percent of it to the ground. When the Germans retreated months later, the Red Army rolled into a deserted ruin, the remains of one of the world's liveliest cities.

The architectural glories one sees now were reconstructed from a series of historic paintings by the Italian master Canaletto, hidden during the war. The entire downtown is an astonishing rebuild. Given the Communist administration's typically brute approach to civic design, it is scarcely imaginable that they executed this makeover, so credit where it's due.

It's a soft stroll to *Stare Miasto*, the Old Town Square, spared from destruction by virtue of its being a historic German merchants' district, now packed with cheerful restaurants and cafés. Taking a tip from some young Lithuanians, we joined them in an eating place—and what outstanding gastronomic delights! Baked goose perogies, hot mulled wine, borsht soup, heaps of mashed potatoes, cabbage salad, rich coffee, and thick apple pie. The Poles eat like the Irish: not fancy, but all quality—beets and pickled cabbage salad with practically everything.

In the cafés, everyone usually speaks some English. *Dobry.* At an interesting spot beside an art gallery, we join Conrad, a professor friend from Lisbon. As we catch up, I can't help glancing at the gallery window. Art posters on sale from Poland's cool film scene of the Andrzej Wajda years in the 1960s and '70s. Originals, bargain prices.

"You can't ignore politics in this country," Conrad says intently, adjusting his glasses. "You will read for sure about the current Right-wing government in Poland; however, it still has Leftist tendencies. There's still something for the Solidarity people; there has to be. However, neoliberalism is over." We will hear this from others too. "History here is still contentious," our friend observes. "The current moment is a balancing act between democracy and populism."

Across Eastern Europe, one country after another has been electing populist, or conservative, nationalist-first governments. Left-of-centre mavens in the arts and academic life in North America and Western Europe look on with alarm. They've grown used to winning in cultural politics, and mired in their present ideology of petty grievance, it's a struggle for them to comprehend the existential anxiety of Poles, Hungarians, Czechs, Estonians, and others faced with globalization, an influx of non-European immigration, or the *diktats* of a central EU bureaucracy in Brussels that frequently rubs against traditional social values. While many Poles look on in alarm as well, Leftist sympathies are in flight here and nationalism is rising; religion is still powerful too, especially in Poland. Authoritarian governments are nothing new when people want security.

That afternoon, we walk through a forest on the city's outskirts. Trees are fairly small; a thin litter of leaves covers the ground. Deer are not uncommon, and Poland's forests, Conrad says, are home to elk and wood bison. The bison serves as an iconic image for the country's favourite Dubrovka vodka, which has a strand of bison grass in each bottle. We walk on through an orderly humdrum housing estate. Magpies congregate in cleared spaces, also the grey, or hooded, crow. Red squirrels in this region have long pointy curved ears—"like Squirrel Nutkin," Kwan-shik says.

Returning by metro, Conrad points out protest banners that call for demonstrations against the government: "teachers, taxi drivers and others want more money," he translates. "Farmers want more subsidies and equality of earning power with teachers and professors."

The Monte Cassino monument at Plac Bankowy honours the Free Polish Army under General Anders who stormed the peak and earned undying renown during the Italian Campaign in WWII. An architect friend back home has crafted a photomontage in memory of his father who served as jeep driver to General Duch, and we've promised to deliver this to the monument. We leave my friend's tribute on the steps with a Remembrance poppy.

Setting off again, Conrad gazes across a broad avenue to a series of tall buildings, part of the new city, and tells us, "That was the old Jewish ghetto that rose up against the Germans in 1943. Completely destroyed. The SS set up its headquarters there."

Back in the metro, he relates that the stylish art deco tiles in Swietokrzyska station are the work of celebrated Polish graphic artist Wojciech Fangor. The square plates feature hip, angular designs in yellow, red, and black—actually thin, microdot printed metal sheets. "They could come straight off a film poster," Kwan-shik reckons.

For years in Vancouver, I tried without success to locate a filmmaker friend, Darek, whom we met in the Himalayas in the mid-eighties. Two days before our departure, a note arrives from another Polish friend in Silesia. Zofia, our Polish Sherlock Holmes, has found Darek. I send a fast letter and attach the single photograph we have of us all, three decades ago.

> We hope you remember our meeting on the hill-train to Darjeeling. Later, we saw you again in Pokhara. When I was ill, you and your friend came to see me at our small hotel with a bottle of Nepali brandy and a piece of yak milk cheese. It probably helped to save my life. We've always remembered your great spirit on the road.

Two days in, we meet for a reunion with bear hugs. Darek is a businessman now. We've all aged, have thicker middles, and a few wrinkles, yet it feels as if we've seen each other not long ago. He drives us in his SUV, and we talk. Life has been good. He works in supply-chain management for restaurants and fast-food operations. Poland, he informs us, was quick to embrace U.S. and Western European business when the liberation came in '89. Plenty of major outfits established East European headquarters and production facilities there. The resulting boom has been significant. Poland's agricultural sector now supplies food chains throughout the continent. Life is better; people from poorer countries want to emigrate here.

"And your film; did you ever complete it? We'd love to see it."

"Well, there's a story…"

We drive to a park where his former classmate, a culinary star with his own television program, has launched a new restaurant. En route, Darek comments how there was no money in making films: "We told the government that we were making a science documentary in Austria, educational stuff. Nobody is mad at Austria, right? We got our permission to travel, six of us.

"Once we left the country, we totally switched plans and bought cheap tickets to India instead. We figured it was the cheapest place to stay away from home for the longest period of time! That was the real plan," he shrugs. "That's when you met us. We'd just flown in."

Darek's team was forced to progressively sell off their European winter clothes and spare film equipment to help finance each leg of their improbable journey through the mountains. They were never without a bottle of booze, and they loved to share. It was impossible not to admire them. "And the documentary?" I asked.

"Ah, the film, yes. It never got finished. We ran out money, someone kept the stock in their basement, and it was ruined in a flood, although I think we may have some still photographs."

Darek introduces us to his wife and daughter when they arrive from work. It's a dinner of rediscovery, blarney, and happy thoughts of the present and the future. A fine thread of Asian connections links us. Darek's sons live abroad where they work with Syrian refugees. He's raised a conscious family, and we can see that they are happy, exactly the right people. They drop us off at the Harenda, and we drift off with the warmest feelings of gratitude in the world. *Dobry.*

Rockin' in the Free World

Conrad invites us for a barbeque; a visiting scholar from Tblisi, Georgia, will come to do some cooking too. After driving through a 700-year-old village outside of town, we indulge in an afternoon party with home-made nettle soup from the garden, and Conrad's own Tokay-style wine from grapevines in his yard. There's vodka, and a tasty Georgian spinach hummus. By the time the hard stuff comes around, Conrad has cranked up his Chinese knockoff model vintage Les Paul and is rocking guitar chords and soloing on British blues.

"Does he know you're packing your harmonica?" Kwan-shik jokes, and then I'm wailing behind him in a once-and-for-all Iron Curtain-smashing blues jam. Lanky Conrad lets it howl, and his neighbours and friends are up dancing. Somewhere in his solo, you can hear Sonny Boy Williamson's "Bring It On Home," and we belt out the tune in rave-from-the-grave style, just a couple of blues guys working toward world peace.

Kwan-shik looks out the window and announces that it is snowing. In April? Yes. We make coffee in our room and have pastries bought the night before. Darek appears again to take us to Powazki Cemetery for the nation's heroes. Last night, when we spoke of the renowned journalist Ryszard Kapuściński, Darek's wife mentioned that her father, a military man, is interred near Kapuściński, and while visiting her dad there recently, she'd passed the grave of our old friend, which she faithfully described. They'd be happy to lead us to it. We drive past scores of flower-sellers; off to pay respects and to say a prayer in memory.

Since discovering him in *Granta* magazine in the early 1980s, I've taught Kapuściński's work to students. We read him in translation, and his reports from Africa and the developing world for the Polish New Service came as a fresh wind, his reporting style unique. Within his reports, there was always a detectable suggestion of similar dark situations in Poland, the Soviet Bloc. How did he get away with it? By being the best. Nobody wrote like him.

We wander the cemetery, past gravestones of every sort. In homage, I am carrying one of Ryszard's letters. Knowing of my interest in the Far East, he once wrote expressing his views on Taoism, stating that "it is such a beautiful, profound, wise and sound...philosophy." He claimed he found it "always a source of joy" and that he felt closer to Taoism than to Confucius. That was Kapuściński all right, avoiding bureaucracy, big bosses. We walk and find his stone marker engraved with a globe of the world. Other readers make this journey; like me they are drawn to the resting places of literary heroes. It's only a quick descriptive, but in homage to one of the greats who took time from a busy life to write an announcement notice for one of my books, I note:

At Kapuściński's Grave
Trzeba Być Dobrym Dla Ludzi
"You have to be good for the people"
Pinsk 4.III.1932-Warsawa 23.1.2007

A jar of pens, dried flowers;
a globe engraved inlay on black stone.
Trees, flowers; bare limbs just coming into bud.
Snowed this morning in April;
Our friend has brought us.
There's peace in this place now,
Far from our home
bird calls, red squirrels twitching.

In an interview with Bill Bruford, Kapuściński stated that his enduring interest was in "the forest of things, as I've seen it, living and travelling in it..."

As we return through the cemetery, I think of his words. He understood the Asian mantra, "No mud, no Lotus." How even from the grimy pond bottom something pure can grow. He knew that trouble makes a good story, especially somebody else's. He'd sussed out the fuller wisdom of the old writer's proverb, "Tell me a story I want to be part of."

Kapuściński's narratives are deceptively colloquial; they embody his understanding of how both the moral and the corrupt can coexist. This is central to his style in which he places himself in dangerous places and situations repeatedly. Punctuated by short jabbing sentences, his reportage comes with a rub of literary license in delivering what Tom Wolfe might call "a larger truth than is possible through the mere compilation of verifiable facts."

Darek indicates a column of young people on a field trip: "Israeli students touring the old Jewish ghetto. Israel brings almost every child to see Poland, to study what happened to Jews in Europe. He leads us across the Vistula to the east bank. It's edgier—grotty shop fronts, Turkish delis, art galleries, bars. It's the cheap side of town, but beginning to gentrify. Then it's sayonara time. We call in for a goodbye with his daughter, waving to them all. We've only just met again after so many years.

In Warsaw, why are we always in tears?

Before heading south, we head for the Chopin salon. Szymon Ogryzek, the pianist, is a Chopin lookalike—longish hair, a passionate attack at the piano. The violinist, Zuzanna Budzynska, is brilliant in a red bare-shouldered ballgown with a small gold cross at her throat. Tracing the high notes as spritely as an alpine stream, she searches for transcendence in the music. By the second work, her playing is stormy, emotional. Their third piece is a pounding scherzo—*Wham! Bomp!*—all in the ambiance of a compact salon with its gleaming Bluthner grand and knowledgeable audience. In Warsaw the whole town is a music academy. Then it's into a familiar Polonaise. Is there another town in the world with such a sophisticated sense of the ephemeral?

After the show, we spot a perogie palace over the road, unpretentious, and there's a table free. We stop counting at thirty-nine varieties and decide it's easiest to order Granny's Special, a combo of fried sausage, cabbage salad, and bread. With a flagon of ale, *Nazdrowie!*

Sunday morning, we cab to the Central Railway Station. It's a well-run facility, spic-and-span, with courteous staff and security, and an efficient

Paul's café from France. On the departure platform, we meet a pair of travellers from India and help them make their connections: Polish is a tricky language.

From a southbound window, Poland's long agricultural vistas look fertile. Unfortunately, this has made it ideal cavalry and tank country. In Silesia, the landscapes are reminiscent of West Yorkshire—Huddersfield, Hebden Bridge, Bradford: brick smokestacks, walls stained by a century of burning coal. We're in the heartland of the European coalfields; the requisite blocks and towers of worker flats stand amid groves of bare deciduous trees.

Sosnowiec is an ordinary Central European town, its buildings three or four stories high. We book into The Centrum adjacent to the railway station. There's an appealing café and a statue in front that looks uncannily like James Joyce chasing his hat. The café exterior is a pale green, and with its painted vines and tables and chairs out front, it could be provincial France.

Rates are lower than Warsaw. We've asked for an electric kettle to make tea and coffee, a seasoned traveller's essential that has yet to catch on throughout Europe. The receptionist asks if we've heard of Jan Kiepura.

"Not so far..."

"There's a statue of him near the station," she says, handing us a local information sheet. Kiepura was a singing star from Sosnowiec, a hometown Jewish boy. In the 1920s, he embarked on a showbiz career in Hungary, Germany, France, and England. His fame exploded, and he made a dozen popular films, starring in everything from opera to comedies. In Warsaw the crowds went wild, and he sang from the balcony of the Hotel Bristol and declaimed for his fans from the roofs of cars parked in Warsaw streets. Then came the Nazis, and he was forced to flee with his wife to New York. Our desk clerk clicks on a YouTube post of Kiepura singing: "He was loved by everyone and had many women," she tells us wistfully. "With them, I think, he could do anything..."

We wait for our key as the desk clerk daydreams. Every morning we are greeted by her, and by the chambermaids, with a smile and friendly *dzień dobry*—"jin-dobry"; it's an all purpose howdy, howya doing? *Dobry.* Kwan-shik, the Pacific linguist says, "*Dobry* means 'aloha.'"

We set off with our professor chum Zofia for the shrine of the Black Madonna of Czestochowska, the holiest shrine in Poland. In warm sun, we cover sixty kilometres over a woody plateau. Here and there, modern operational towers thrust upward atop coalmine shafts and smokestacks, adding to the sooty air. The countryside is tame with clusters of homes built around older relics. The land is unusually gentle, and we've no need to hurry. The sacred image of the Black Madonna and child in green, gold, blue, and dark orange will be unveiled for the faithful at a Palm Sunday afternoon mass in the Basilica.

Being blessed on Palm Sunday is a special way to experience Silesia and Poland. I'm not sure what to expect, but the walled monastery of Jasna Góra, founded by Pauline monks in 1382, is large and imposing. Its fame was kick-started in 1655 when invading Swedes besieged the monastery unsuccessfully for forty days. Thus began the legend of the Black Madonna, Protector of Poland. Pilgrims come from throughout the country, often walking for weeks.

Zofia is familiar with the protocols and guides us around the hill-top site. We view its chapels, armoury, museum with religious treasures, and a room full of abandoned crutches and artificial limbs left by the miraculously healed. Outside the monastery gate, we join a procession of pilgrims walking up the cobbled way, mainly young people, and many young priests in red vestments, as well as the archbishop with his crook and tall mitre hat. Others carry speaker packs and broadcast hymns for the faithful to join in. How rare to be among those who openly demonstrate their faith. We don't walk a long way before attending a homily from the Archbishop. Zofia translates: "We have to be tolerant. He's encouraging people to be forgiving, to overcome homophobia, to remain strong in their faith. He's explaining to the young that to be of faith can mean being ridiculed."

Catholicism is embedded here, although fading with modernity in larger cities. Inside the chapels, masses are said all day long this Holy Week. Next we enter the basilica, its lighting dim. The ancient walls have withstood everything—Swedes, Turks, Hitler and the Germans, Stalin and the Russians. A familiar fragrance of beeswax candles and incense lingers in the air. Beneath the stained glass windows, people are on their knees, devout in their expression of faith. They have kept their sacred traditions. Grown men and women, fashionable teenagers, everyone is in prayer, contemplating their solemn communion with the Black Madonna. I'm surprised by how near to her image above the altar we are able to draw. The crowds of pilgrims self-organize; everyone is assured of some personal time near the holy image.

A nudge at my sleeve, and I'm pointed toward a processional passageway around the high altar. It is paved of uneven cobblestones, worn smooth through the centuries by the knees of pilgrims. Silently we join the processional. It's a meditation that swiftly becomes a penance, with my knees shouting for relief. A handrail proves its worth. But the next day, I'm miraculously fine, although the toes of my shoes are well-scraped and dusty, officially a pilgrim's. At Czestochowska, I witness something fundamental from old Poland and feel kinship with these people. In alliance with the Duchy of Lithuania next door, their nation was once a European power in this boxy geographic splinter of the world; it has stories as magical as anybody's—of King Casimir and Esterka, his sweet Jewish lover who helped him bring beneficence to her community.

The modern world is rapidly losing this deep public sense of communion, although Indigenous peoples still retain it with their profound connection to the Earth and their traditional territories. The Silesians, about one million of them, have their own distinct dialect and regard themselves as indigenous keepers of their territory.

When I show my documentary film and speak at the university in Sosnowiec, a campus of the University of Silesia, the event is well-organized and well-attended. It goes without a hitch. Students ask about the Burning Man Festival and San Francisco's counterculture scene in the sixties, a question I was also asked in Warsaw. "We want to rediscover our roots and traditions from before the Christians—*the mystery, the mysterious*," an articulate, longhaired young man says. "The mystery" emerges as a constant topic of conversation with these educated young, the desire for communion with the divine, with a higher, deeper sense of grace. Has Van Morrison been singing here? It's a pleasure grooving among such committed, engaged young adults. *Dobry.*

We pop into a teashop like something from the English dales. Good coffee, glass cases of thick cream cakes made in the back. The seating is an eclectic mix of armchairs and tea tables. We talk literature, what's going on in the journals and newspapers about Ukraine, which lives in the shadow of Vladimir Putin. Two million Ukrainians live in Poland now, and two million Poles emigrated west in Europe to work in France, Ireland, Britain. "No Yin without a Yang" my old Taoist master used to say.

Several students and professors say that Ukraine is close to chaos. With an election underway, they are about to vote for a comedian as president. Is it coincidence that Surrealism and Absurd Art produced so many personalities from East and Central Europe—Ionesco, Tzara, Kafka, Moholy-Nagy? They practically invented it.

At Katowice, the regional capital and customary last stop before visits to Auschwitz up the road, we walk toward the town centre. Poland's universities earn high ratings internationally and are a nexus for young scholars from nations we hear little of—Latvia, Armenia, Turkey, Bulgaria, and Kaliningrad, that strange tranche of territory the Russians hold between Lithuania and Poland, formerly Konigsberg in East Prussia. Katowice is bustling—this is where the World Forum on Climate Systems Change was just held, not far from the coalfields.

In the public square's Easter Market, the open-air food and beer stalls are sensational—heaps of smoked sausages and salamis, tasty cheeses, crusty loaves of hearth bread. Zofia joins us and offers to take us to her hometown, Zory. Somehow we detour and stop first to meet her friends in a coal miners' village. It's quiet and the air has an acrid tang. The country is still a massive producer of both hard black and softer dirty brown lignite coal—the major polluter—that can be surface strip-mined. The family welcomes us in, and the father with a thick Pilsudski moustache brings out a cask of his clear homemade white lightning. The mother slices a plate of lard sandwiches, and we sit in the formal parlour, where after a prayer of thanks, we work at a conversation. Zofia explains that her friend is a poet, and with eyes closed, the mother recites us a poem, then another. We're newcomers here, but you don't have to tell us she's a spiritual poet; the faith exudes from her. Then she sings and we're laughing, knocking back shots of the bone-crushing liquor. *Dobry!* My turn now—one must have a song from your own country handy—and I pipe up with "The Parting Glass." Haven't we all been a bit foolish in our time and wiser now?

It's a short, soulful meeting, then we're off with another stop at what Zofia says locals call "The Road of Martyrs." You can choose not to go to Auschwitz as we've done; but there's no escaping the wartime killing fields. Zofia played near this spot of woodland as a kid, she says. Always it was a sad place, "but our ball would roll over there."

She pulls up besides a thin stretch of forest, and we walk to a cairn in memory of thirty-nine inmates of Auschwitz who were driven here and murdered. Why here? "The Red Army was closing in. Every town in this region was shot up. Truckloads of prisoners were driven off," our friend says, "perhaps dreaming of release. There are sites like this all over the wartime area of the camps." An inscription honours the murdered Jews, with an unmistakable series of numbers in lieu of names, taken from the tattoos borne by each prisoner. No guided tour necessary. Everything unendurable is said, even that left unsaid.

In Krakow a musician insists we eat in a milk-bar restaurant, and we wisely take her suggestion. These former state-subsidized cafés dish up decent food; some are exquisitely decorated in traditional Polish needlepoint design, and you can enjoy one of the best meals of your life for about five dollars.

Krakow is a medieval market town with stupendous architecture, and we're blown away by its beauty. Culture matters here. At St. Mary's Church, the Trumpeter of Krakow still sounds his call in person every hour—now there's a legend for you. Turn up Grodzka Street toward Wawel Hill, and you'll find the country's national symbol of sovereignty, a generously spread out, thick-walled castle.

We walk the greenbelt around the city's inner core, wandering past historic Jagiellonian University. It's an easy stroll then up Ulica Stradomska to the old Kazimierz Jewish Quarter. We wander up Miodowa Street, and there's a little lace embroidery shop near an old synagogue. An embroidery of endearing red poppies, a favourite emblem in Poland, costs a dollar and a half. Small shops of handmade clothing, shawls, and housewares appear. It's the beginnings of the district. Already I feel like we're in a story by Isaac Bashevis Singer.

On compact Szeroka Street, you don't have to be Jewish to stand there and breathe in the vibes for one precious moment, or to imagine what it must have been like, the nightmare. So this too, is part of our pilgrimage.

"This part of town was neglected, run-down," a young woman selling mezuzahs next to the old Jewish cemetery explains. "Now the small hotels are being bought and renovated with Jewish names and atmosphere." The area is reimagining itself as the city's bohemian quarter. Schindler's Factory is a few minutes away on Lipowa Street, and in summertime the Jewish Cultural Festival has the whole town jumping.

I think of what Kapuściński might say—a writer who wanted to know the truth for what it is; how this story rests "at the centre of the forest of things." *Polska.* An old culture that insists on hearing its voice in the places it knows as its own.

Dzień dobry.

2019

OLD JEWISH QUARTER, KRAKOW POLAND

LIVING THE ARTIST'S LIFE IN MADRID

SPAIN

Slim and I were headed for Lisbon. Spain was one of those things that happen on the road, left instead of right. Freud says there are no coincidences, but that's how I ended up staying near Madrid with the artists Marcos Irizarry and Abel Bello at Calle San José #1, in what was then still the small town of Pozuelo d'Alarcón Estación.

My guitar buddy, Slim, and I were young musicians, and we played the blues. In the early '70s, after a rainy fortnight in London, we'd sized up our options. The greasy flagstones underfoot and the English fog and drizzle had got to us, and no amount of Soho's Wardour Street action would relieve it, even the nights when Rod Stewart still sang with the Faces at The Marquee, the best club in the country. One night, a grifter in a Leicester Square pub put us wise to Lisbon—"best cheap digs and cutest girls in the South," he said. Well, that was it, wasn't it? In the late sixties, before the U.S. collapse in Southeast Asia, before Watergate, you could live all winter in Portugal on what they charged for a month and a half in a Bayswater bedsit. So said Nairobi Ted.

We set off, thumbing to the Dover boat. Three rides later, we stared at Canterbury Cathedral. Chaucer filled my imagination with his *Tales* that we'd been forced to read chained to a desk in high school. Wasn't this the spot where the saintly archbishop was slaughtered on his altar?

Richard Burton and Peter O'Toole educated us about this in *Becket,* and the high Anglican T.S. Eliot wrote a play about it—*Murder in the Cathedral.* Leavened with a sense of providence, we moved on in our meditations. "There's no road without adventure," my father used to say.

Bad weather followed like an Irish curse, and outside Calais across the Channel, we bummed a lift to Boulogne in filthy rain. We'd only just arrived in France, and already, fast-moving Slim was growing antsy. Then a crazy break: Our search for dry shelter turned up an abandoned gypsy caravan, broken and leaky, but a haven nonetheless in the sodden dark. We rolled out our sleeping bags and crashed, hoping for the best.

By half past ten the next morning, we were coughing on the raw streets of Paris, looking for a train. "O for a beaker full of the warm South..." I grumbled.

"Bob Dylan?"

"Keats for gawdsakes..."

"Man, bring on the southern climes," Slim groused, staring darkly. His guitar case slapped against his leg. I noticed his boot heels wouldn't stand much more tramping.

After the Paris grunge of Gare du Nord, we climbed down from a railcar in Bordeaux within striking distance of the Pyrénées, where without the least prior connection, we met a tribe of student Maoists. *Vive la révolution!* Such were the times: You whipped out your harmonica, your buddy flashed his guitar; you cranked out "Got My Mojo Working" and hoped for the best. So it goes. After a night of hard drinking in the very cradle of French plonk, we landed a night on the floor in some leftist student digs. Come morning, we were rousted out by our comrade hosts with a quick toke and scarcely a word of *au revoir*. I glanced at sultry photos of Julie Greco and Jean Seberg—existential pinups of the time—as we thumped out the door. *Vive la révolution!*

Back on the streets, we trekked to a hayseed country crossroads and stood banjaxed for hours. "We can't buy a ride," Slim groused. "Not even the prayer method works. We're hooped." With a thing for tight sweaters, he moaned about the cheerleader he'd left back home.

Stamping our feet, we watched the frost on our breath as a river of vehicles swept by for hours without mercy. The sun fell. Soon the snow came falling softly, impossibly white like night on the blue Pacific. My gloves had disappeared, and my hands were numb. Slim sat on his knapsack, fumbling with his guitar case. Lisbon with its sunshine seemed a long way away. Our funds were tight. France was costly, yet Slim nagged for finding a room and a hot meal. I held close to the highway's shoulder, thumb out. Another hour passed. Slim grew despondent: "We're crazy, bumming a lift in the black of night in a strange country."

Out of nowhere, headlights pulled up down the road. A well-worn Citroen, French plates. It slumped to the left as if the shocks needed attention. I ran to check if the lift was real. Drawing close, I saw the woman driver looking me over. We spoke through the window; our bum's luck held. I yelled back to Slim, "She's driving through to the frontier then, on through Spain to Madrid. Seven hundred kilometers! Let's move it!"

The driver backed up the shoulder, looked Slim over pitifully, nodded, and we tossed our packs aboard. The Citroen bumped on down the road. And so our journey began.

"O merciful Buddha!"

"I am Francoise," our benefactor said, eyes on the road. We gave our names. Communication would have to be *en français.* She was mossy-haired, dressed in winter black, thick glasses, leather boots. We spoke in French, and she told us her story; I translated as best I could for Slim curled up in the back. With the mountains ahead and a frontier to cross, we talked through the night for hours—Vietnam, the War, Sartre, René Char, Canada, and Quebec. She'd been a student in Madrid, fell in love with a painter, and had been yanked back home "for her own good" by her family, she explained. As much I could fathom, her angry father was a vestigial minor aristocrat of the *ancien régime.* Now she was running away, leaving France, rejoining her lover in Spain for good.

"*Vrai romantique...*"

"She's got heart. You have to like her," I said to Slim as we drove on in the darkness with the slack suspension bringing a bruise with every bump. It grew later, and we approached the hill country, then began rising up wintery, treacherous grades into the Pyrénées. The headlights exposed previous snowbanks two or three feet deep, and already fresh flakes blew around us. Slim was out to the world; I carried on conversation as best as I could with Francoise until, at two AM, the motor crapped out, deader than the ghost of Christmas-yet-to-come. We were stalled in the dark with a blizzard flying hard around us now and an engine that wouldn't kick over.

Slim woke up: "What's happening?" We dragged him out. He stood looking around at the scene, slapping his hands together. "Flip the hood," he groused.

Slim looked over the motor. He tried cranking the engine. Pulling a red bandana from his duffel pocket, he wiped down the fuel line and tapped it a few times. Minutes later he was sucking hard and spewing gob-fulls of gasoline. Groaning distaste for the whole enterprise, he wiped his mouth with a clean edge of cloth, and croaked, "Fire it up."

Damned if it didn't spark. "Amigo, you're a mechanical genius! What'd you do?"

"Not a lot. Rust in the gas tank. In this weather we'll need a truck stop and a few tools before long, if we make it that far..."

An hour later we saw lights through the snow, an all-night trucker's pullout. Francoise hauled in; we drank strong coffee and sat out the blizzard with serious men who looked like bandit cutthroats. Then Slim got up gesturing, walking around the tables. Who knew that he understood motors? A trucker led him out and loaned him a few tools "to swab out the filter. It's not rocket science." With *mercis* and *gracias* all around, a half-hour later we slogged back into the storm.

We struggled on for another hour and a quarter. Francoise was exhausted; she'd driven all day from Troyes. With no point in pushing danger, we stopped at a pull-over, and lowered the car seats to grab some snooze, while outside the snow blew wet and furious. Tossing in the freezing cold, I saw the hazard lights of road crews flashing through our windows as they ploughed the alpine road in the dark.

At the frontier in early daylight, Francoise eased us through customs and immigration speaking good Spanish, and we had our entry stamps. Anxious to reach her lover, she led us for a walkabout to stretch our legs in San Sebastian. We ate oily sausage and fresh warm bread at the first café we saw open, and then pushed toward Burgos and on to the capital.

The late rising sun brought us a first clear look at the Basque country, stark and powerful.

Taking a break to change money at a cambio, we saw the Guardia Civil in their 18th century helmets swagger by with machine guns. "Don't look at them," Francoise whispered. "Give no excuse for confrontation."

"No problem…"

Motoring onward, Francoise told us about the ETA, the Basque guerillas who regularly struck against Franco. *El Caudillo*, she informed, was no friend of the Basques.

"I will leave you at the best stop for Portugal," Francoise said with a sideways shrug of her head. We were headed due south.

"Then it's good we'll be swinging straight past the big bossman's city without stopping," twanged Slim, listening in as best he could. Francoise gave him a look in her rearview mirror. "Perfect time for a travelling song," Slim smiled, tuning his guitar. We were on the road again.

The silence in Irun was unnerving, like a futuristic movie. The city felt deserted, its Sunday morning streets empty; nothing moved, not even the birds were chirping. Driving cautiously through shadowy streets, we made for what looked to be the Madrid road, rounding a blind corner ready to hit the throttle.

The cannon barrel of the tank pointed dead at our windscreen, its gravity brutally convincing. Military personnel, flares, and barricades were everywhere. Efficient men in uniform with guns pulled us over to the roadside, snapping directions.

"They're saying 'Out of the car. *Now.*'"

They frisked us, asked for our passports, searched thoroughly. It happened quickly; questions barked with hard authority. Francoise stumbled in answer, explained who we were—as best she knew. Soldiers shook down the car, rooted through our sacks. It was a hell of a welcome to holy Spain, land of bullfights and fiestas.

"Hey!" Slim hollered at one soldier to be careful with his guitar. A sharp, belligerent look silenced him. We were meant to be scared.

Led into a guard post, cold, functional, we sat as khaki-uniformed men stomped by. They had our passports. We wondered what came next. Too nervous to speak, we waited apprehensively, listening to the crackle of a radio wireless. I had a hard, dull headache. Francoise smoked cigarettes for the first time since we'd met.

An officer in olive-green presented himself, snapping at Francoise in rapid Spanish. Then, abruptly, they released us without apology or explanation. She was badly shaken.

"I have an international license," I related softly. I'd thought it might be useful.

"Please drive," she said. We switched spots up front. I hit the ignition, stalling the French motor.

"Settle down, settle down," Slim soothed. I tried again, and she fired this time. The Citroen jerked up the road. We kept an eye on the soldiers behind us. "Let's get *outa* here..." In minutes we passed through the outskirts of town. Suddenly, it was country again.

"A bomb exploded near Irun last night," Francoise confided. "They're looking for the ETA. It's the army and they're angry. They demanded to call my family. You guys will be okay, I think, but now my father will know where I am."

Hours went by. We travelled slowly, and the day slipped away. Still rattled, Francoise took some rest and darkness fell. We neared Madrid, and whether it was gratitude for Slim's mechanical skill, or for our company on the road, Francoise volunteered to ask her friends if they'd let us rest until we'd shaken off our dust.

We were bleary-eyed as she pulled the Citroen over beside a white three-storey house in a cobbled lane, then left. Returning minutes later, she quietly told us that we could bunk on the top floor. We followed her up flights of steps to a large bare storehouse skirted with tall wooden racks and dropped our packs. Francoise shrugged, smiling. "You can sleep here," she said, then disappeared.

Our breath made clouds in the chilly air. The lower racks would make decent bunks. Exhausted, we threw down our sleeping bags and crashed in our clothes.

Spain was a poor country in those times. Unless you had money, Madrid wasn't especially glamorous. Generalissimo Franco and his fascist Falange still held absolute power thirty years after the terrible civil war that had served as a prelude to WWII, and life, or the way you spoke of it, was restricted for anyone of liberal opinion.

Pozuelo d'Alarcón had its own curious draw. It was still a quiet, distinct community ten kilometres away from the capital. Geraldine Chaplin, the actress of *Dr. Zhivago* fame, lived in a large private house with property not far off, and Orson Welles had lived there with his Italian actress wife, Paola Mori. Since then, the farmland between Pozuelo and the capital has disappeared, and the old village has been absorbed as a trendy neighbourhood within greater Madrid, but back then more chickens than celebrities still roamed the dusty streets.

The sound of a voice in English woke me. A dream? "How you guys doing? I'm from Seattle..." A tall bearded American looked down at us. "I'm Cameron, welcome to Pozuelo." Then a second figure arrived. "This is Ginger, my wife. We're researchers at the Prado. Friends of the house."

Thus, with this first night's invitation, then another and another, Slim and I began our unexpected sojourn in Madrid. Unbidden, it would alter my perception of life. In Spain there was art, wine, and soul—a different way of living than anything I'd known before. The house at Calle San José was a busy working studio. The core household was comprised of Marcos Irizarry, a printmaker and painter; Abel Bello, also a printmaker and painter; and Paco, a bearded sculptor who remained comparatively remote.

Marcos was from Caribbean Puerto Rico and not yet famous. Abel would consolidate his own career and also achieve recognition; with his younger brother, Manolo, he also undertook fine letterpress work that includes a collector's book edition of Margaret Atwood's *The Journals of Susanna Moodie*. Of the others: Manolo was a part-time visitor; Mitsuo, from Japan, studied sculpture with Paco; as well as Francoise; and a floating cast of lovers, and sojourners like Slim and me. Marcos and Abel were older than me, but Manolo and I were close in age and chummed together. Through him, I came to know Abel. Through Abel, I grew to know his more remote and quieter friend, Marcos. A handful of other foreigners like Cam and Ginger lived nearby, mostly young Americans keeping out of the military during the Vietnam War.

Marcos was the principal actor and managed the big old house. I met him the first morning with Cam. Marcos was perfect in his way: dark, handsome, thin beard. He spoke heavily inflected English and was serious about one thing only, *Art.* He had a curious tic, raising an eyebrow when he spoke. I'd never known a serious painter before, although as a boy I'd watched my father construct a painstaking mosaic mural of Mount Fuji for a job out of thousands of tiny tiles.

Marcos was strong, committed, honest; a little vulnerable perhaps, but never forceful. He looked you in the eyes, sizing you up. After meeting Cam, I'd followed him downstairs where I found Marcos unaffected, intimidating. You knew there was no putting anything over on this man.

The studio house was much like him; the same cool beat. Mornings, the household rose with frost on the blankets to dress and make its way to the bodega down the lane for strong coffee and cheap 501 brandy, the Spanish restorative to the lungs. If you had a little money, you could buy small plates of *tapas*—egg tortilla, spiced octopus, bits of liver.

Through the day, the men worked steadily. The house consisted of a series of working studios. Paco occupied the street-level space with high ceilings where a massive Styrofoam and plaster-covered megalith after Henry Moore was in advanced stage for bronze casting. Marcos and Abel shared a hand-cranked printing press to produce their serigraphs. This process fascinated me, and I spent hours watching and studying the mechanics of their labour. Other than the sounds of the press, the silence of the house seemed at odds with their work—with Marcos's ochre symbols, or Abel's loud dramatic abstracts. The atmosphere was serious by day with no allowance for triflers. It was best to vacant the premises and leave them to their devices, though they made allowance for visits, explanation, and elucidation.

In the small kitchen, a wall-mounted water geyser hung above the sink; the *baño* next to it completed affairs with the first bidet I'd laid eyes on. The loft above was freezing most of the time and occasionally housed smoked hocks, jars of olives, wine, and unexpected guests like us.

It was in the evening over large communal dinners that the house came alive, that the magic occurred, and spells were cast that affected so many. These were times for the shaping of lives. After long days of work, the artists downed their tools and the matter of preparing dinner commenced. Everyone took a turn, helping cook or clean up one night; and in reverse order the next, a cheerful undertaking with girlfriends especially active. Meals were simple and delicious—risotto, paella, and spaghetti, one-pot dinners that fed many mouths. If you had limited skills like mine, you learned. Abel or one of the others gave instructions—what kind of rice you need for risotto, which olives are good on the side.

Sticks of bread and hearth loaves from the baker, along with bottles of local *rioja,* cost pennies. Conversation in Spanish, English, French, whatever was sparkling, brilliant, full of opinions—always art, travel, news of faraway places, philosophy, democracy, the coming and goings of friends and rivals, announcements of gallery exhibitions. Then, with the plates cleared, music—deep, passionate, topical. In Spain, who didn't have a guitar? Everyone around the table or sitting against the wall joined in to sing or play, and they expected that you'd offer a song from your region.

During this winter, I discovered the possibility of living the artist's life, what it takes internally, psychologically, and what that kind of ongoing life that entails—not Hollywood's version of solitary geniuses brooding above the sea, or art school dropouts that self-dramatize the lifestyle; this was honest goods, a chance to witness what it takes to wake up and face life without a steady paycheque, to face the day ahead in hope of creating something worth the trouble—that might sell, or at least earn respect from valued peers, without upsetting the neighbours. The members of the household unconsciously demonstrated these lessons every day in their continual practice of self-discipline, faith in their enterprise, comradely sharing, and generosity. I have never forgotten these lessons and have only rarely seen or heard of them in formal institutional settings.

Through conversations with Marcos, I came to understand that he came by his skills diligently. He'd studied intaglio printing in Puerto Rico, then Madrid, and explained that he was working "toward a synthesis of Caribbean and European influences in my work." He was acquainted with New York's expressionist school then in heavy vogue, but it had no particular influence on his thinking. Rather, he'd acquired a classical training and, by the early 1950s, was exploring his passion for Goya.

Goya was always there, and in Marcos's early work, there's the obvious natural influence of this mentor figure. He also travelled, though not to the likeliest destinations. Instead, he'd visit Prague and Yugoslavia to meet other artists and intellectuals. He did this during the deep chill of the Cold War era, when any travel behind the Iron Curtain assured a *frisson* of nervous energy. I'm unsure if he physically saw Albania near Tito's more liberal Yugoslavia, but I recall he and Abel talking animatedly about the Albanians, their primitive traditions—"wild, long-haired people; they love riding horses." The Albanians had a zest for blood feuds too, something that perhaps struck a chord with the Spaniards. During the conversation, Abel, with his thin cheeks and bushy sideburns, pulled out a thin dagger, a weapon forbidden by the Guardia Civil. It was ornately engraved and had hollows in the blade: "It introduces air into the bloodstream, kills more quickly that way," he explained professorially.

Lively discussion regarding knives, daggers, and Toledo steel led Marcos to bring up an occasion in France. While travelling with his amigos, for some reason or other the police had intervened. On learning that Irizarry and the rest were Spaniards, the gendarmes stepped back, demanding they produce their weapons on the spot.

"What!" Irizarry demanded.

"Your knives. You're Spaniards. You all carry them!" Hilarious laughter all around; more wine.

Marcos bounced around as artists do while looking for the ideal place to work. At an engraving class in '69, where both were workshop associates at the Taller Libre, he met Mitsuo Miura. The pair took up residence in Pozuelo, were joined by Abel, then Paco, creating a fertile environment. Manolo joined the trio on a journey to Sweden where the Bellos also kept a studio. Marcos's abstract geometric style would undergo further transformation through his associations with the Pozuelo group.

Life in Pozuelo reflected the tenor of the times. Around the world, artists, intellectuals, and young people were on the move as the sixties' counterculture project gathered steam. Marcos recognized how the international flow of foreigners and Spanish alike would bring new ideas and energies, new ways of thinking. The studio circle was already open to flamenco and fado music, rock bands, the blues, Archie Shepp, and New

York's wild free jazz elements. Los Bravos, the rock band with its one worldwide hit "Black Is Black," was part of the network of acquaintances, along with the other big Madrid group at the time, Los Canarios.

There too the door opened for me—a little, but sufficiently—to mystical Asia, then extremely remote and exotic. One came into contact with those who had made the long trek to Asia and returned with knowledge in the practice of insight traditions—yoga, meditation, karate. The *Zeitgeist* of the late sixties was permeated with influences from Tibet, from Buddhism, Hindu meditation, Sufi doctrine, and Bahai. Abel had wonderful tales from his Asian days. He'd been to monasteries and told stories about meditation in the snow, relying on *tumo* inner heat, and monks in Ladakh who played metal jaw harps so enormous, he said, they made your entire skull bone resonate. The metal reed was so strong that, if you were careless when you twanged it, it knocked your front teeth out. Abel had brought one back in his knapsack. He would hand you the instrument as a test. You paid *extremely* close attention to what you were doing.

"Good dharma practice," he called it. Young and on the road, we sought intoxication of one kind or another where we could find it. I caught a glimpse of the Himalayas in Abel's stories that he shared in the evenings, and they stayed in my mind as a kind of floating zendo. It seemed important, and in the idealism of those times, a good dharma practice was regarded as an antidote to the sins of the age—the war in Vietnam, the vicious and persistent repression of what had come to be known as the counterculture, the increasing commercialization of society, the emerging environmental crisis, the carceral belligerence of the Cold War, you name it.

"Such sins keep the world in darkness," Abel affirmed.

Marcos and Abel introduced me to their tools and working methods. Most of this was new, but I'd grown up with a stonemason father and worked among craftsmen since I'd been old enough to carry a set of brick tongs. I'd worked at a daily paper too, where relations between writers and shop-floor printers were close. On hearing this, Marcos nodded in agreement, considering it correct, traditional policy. Although he worked alone, he had a collaborative streak and took pleasure in the company of like-minded artists. He was a natural instructor, while still refining particular skills of his own. He subscribed to the belief that art was a liberating impulse. Later, Abel would link this to the work of Jung, contending that art was a reflection of the deeper inner self. Abel had his own associations, the result of his long journeys through the Himalayas.

In a later interview, Marco would say, "Art is a profound manifestation of the particular self of each artist; it has to mature inside you, to get out little by little." Who would argue with that? Well, *everyone*—at least over dinner, before ultimately agreeing it made perfect sense.

One morning at the bodega, several locals were talking with a newspaper seller who regularly held down a chair there. Although he looked like a labourer, the old man was reputedly the richest fellow in Pozuelo. "He's saved every peseta he ever earned and bought land with it for decades around here," Marcos winked. "A millionaire, seriously." The paper seller had one love in his life, a playboy son who raced around in a convertible, chasing women. Given the rough economics of the area, this was regarded as something of an accomplishment. Apart from his fatherly sponsorship, the old man did what he enjoyed best, playing dominoes, drinking a little and watching the *futbol*, and once or twice a month taking home Adèla, the discreet *prostituta* who looked after a widowed mother, and who was relatively well treated by all.

Conversing with the leathery-faced tycoon, Marcos turned. "We should be at the Prado today," he said. Was it something he'd heard from the old geezer? Within a short time, six or seven of us were at the bus stop. This would be the first of our educational excursions.

What a formidable guide Marcos was: Under his tutelage, we spent hours studying first Goya, then Bosch, then sessions on Velázquez and El Greco. After assessing them for us, he urged, "You should go to Toledo. See where El Greco worked to depict his personal experience of faith."

Slim and I would do precisely that, crossing the plain outside of Madrid then on to the promontory of Toledo, cut away steeply on three sides by the River Manzanares. It is hard to ignore the city's history from the Middle Ages onward; in the narrow streets, you encounter figures who could argue their way out of a play by Calderón.

Back at the house, the artists kept working. Marcos was engaged in a connected suite of abstracts he called his Colibri series. He'd pin up the works and explain the method and ethos behind his current imaginings. Umber was the predominant colour; he returned to it time and time again. And always his works had a centre. See them once, and the brownish hues and black lines never left you. His abstracts were sombre; he was a man who saw deeply, and there's no escaping the glimpses of chains or bound figures in his work from this period. In this he drew inspiration from Goya's *Disasters of War*, depicting Spain's struggle against Napolean. Only a moral coward could have ignored the fascist reality of his own time.

Irizarry's work had a brooding totemic element, but a Turtle Islander from North America could recognize it at once; the unmistakable Indigenous Latin American motifs, Andean and Mexican especially—patterns synthesized and reintegrated into his own unique mélange. His strength was in geometric forms, but from our visits to the Prado, I saw him borrow motifs from Bosch. Where for Bosch they brought chaos, Marcos used the ovoid to bring order, containment. His colour schemes in the Colbri are strong and resonant, not yet joyous; he was mining some deeper spring of inspiration, and the colours he worked with are of an Iberian metaphoric landscape.

The critic Walter Benjamin wrote of the role of the political in the framing of modern art, and how it tempers perception. Marcos echoed such ideas with relief prints using white on white, an experiment completely limiting the use of colour. These artists didn't try to make it easy for the viewer.

Later I heard a disturbing report from San Juan. During a visit back to Puerto Rico in the early 1980s, a scant year after he'd been awarded a major prize on the island, he was accosted by police and brutally assaulted during some civil unrest—an act of police-state barbarity. But the Marcos I'd known, while politically conscious, had a mature artist's political savvy: the jumped-up allegations against him didn't wash. For a soul of his introspective nature, to be attacked and terrorized on his native island after twenty years in fascist Spain must have brought incalculable sorrow.

Over the years, word occasionally arrived of Marcos's career and successes. A year after we met, he moved to Ibiza and the blue brilliance of the Mediterranean. His works from this period show how its colours and atmosphere had seeped in, bringing new warmth and joy to his oeuvre. He undertook his first major mural there. During the seventies, he worked in Italy; it was becoming a bastion of ecologically minded European art. Similar to the Bellos, he tackled fine-press book art. In Spain, art, literature, and music are never far apart.

While Marcos steadily moved toward renown, I continued my own journeys. In Mexico I saw my first revolutionary mural by Jose Orozco in Guadalajara. In Mexico City I encountered murals by Diego Rivera and David Siqueiros, and Freida Kahlo's work. They hit like a summertime blast: Marcos's work vibrating back at me.

Time passes. A librarian friend brought news. Marcos had done well, exhibiting in a dozen countries, New York, and California. In 1987, he received academic honour at last, an artist-in-residence appointment at the University of Puerto Rico, Mayagüez, a position he retained until his premature death at 59 in Guaynabo in 1995. His work is now on permanent exhibition in the university gallery.

Slim and I never made it to Lisbon. Instead, we embarked on a road trip south. Ending up broke in Granada, we turned our boots northward for Amsterdam. Manolo fell in love with a girl who sang in a club. Francoise, the sincere lover, returned to France. Abel kept making prints. Paco earned acclaim for his sculpture; and a letter from someone announced that Cameron and Ginger returned to Seattle.

Was our joint venture a success? In the great Pozuelo ledger, the tabulations are kept with a different kind of arithmetic. We would always be contenders, Marcos reckoned, as long as we stayed true to what we loved and believed in. There, I first let go of my religion while embracing a new community of artists and friends. They do things that way in Spain. For fifty years, I've had this love of them all engraved on my heart.

CIRCA 1970

WHERE THREE DREAMS CROSS

BRITISH COLUMBIA

Vancouver summer, early July, and Kwan-shik and I dawdled through the morning, watching overcast skies for any break in the weather. Stir-crazy with inactivity, by one o'clock we made a move. Since a day at the beach was off, we'd try the mountains. An hour and a half later, with only light packs, we were well on the way to Cypress Bowl with its jagged trail to Black Mountain Peak.

With each quarter-hour, the weather grew more mawkish; overripe clouds threatened rain, even thunder. Occasionally, in spots, sunlight pierced the muggy haze, and the prospect of snowcapped ridges ahead made a few mountain hours too tempting to resist. Following a switch-back, we glanced upon the vast metropolis spread below, a vista ranging clear to the American border at Semiahmoo Bay more than twenty miles off.

Farther along, the guttural booms of a big male grouse thumped lonely on the cool, sombre air.

Then we watched, amazed, as a red-tailed hawk powered through the sky at three thousand feet over the alpine valley beyond us, swooping the thermals, working the ridge for prey.

An hour later, we hit summer snowline. A melt-water brook surged from dense brush, and we tramped after it to drink at the clean crystal source. Heading back to the trail, Kwan-shik said she'd feared that a tiger might have jumped us by surprise. All the Orient's best childhood myths involve tigers.

"No need worrying about that," I said, smiling. "There's nothing but mountain lions around this time of year."

Marching higher in the territory of a second booming grouse, we paused to eat a handful of trail mix. A trekker's hut perched on log stilts nearby. Again the grouse boomed, and tracing his calls, we saw him roosting in the crick of a jack pine until he flew off to darker cover.

We set off again, travelling with caution. A shifty patch of trail had been shored-up with rough planking, the thaw holes beneath betraying melt-water rivulets. A wrong step meant a tumble into near-frozen, boggy mush. In poor light, we trucked farther through dense alpine forest, and the wilderness path grew difficult to discern. Trusting the coloured trail tags marked high on guide trees, we pushed patiently onward.

After a last cover of pines, we reached the summit. No signage, no announcement; we simply arrived. Beyond us lay huge horizons. We stood above everything. Occasionally, a small aircraft flew well below us, as turbulent vapours clouded the sun.

Enjoying the rare moment, we sat side by side on the bare granite knoll. Small pine and scrub flecked the summit, and about the edges lay a carpet of moss. Leaving packs aside, we stretched on our backs and gazed up at the show of clouds.

Soon, blackflies were biting. I rose and bundled twigs for a fire that sparked to life on a bare spot of rock. I added damp leaves to make smoke. Opening a flask of tea, we munched on hard-boiled eggs and sweet nectarines. All around us, profound stillness. Eyes half-closed, we lay back again, so much nearer heaven.

We must have dozed, for soon the light declared it was time to descend. Setting off, we hacked down to the west as a low golden light reflected off the ridges. We saw it then while stumbling onto an unkempt clearing. Simultaneously struck speechless, we caught our breath, moved nearer the apocryphal vision.

Before us lay a spectacular bowl, the natural convergence of three snow-clad peaks. The setting sun now trained on this remote open space, while boiling upward through the ethers an ocean of vapours surged forth, rising formlessly, opalescent, pulsing with life. Furling and unfurling, cloud-hidden to the world, the immutable void of a hundred ancient parables danced before us, a kind of volcanic updraft of primordial Chi, ceaselessly merging and re-emerging in fantastic whorls of energy. We looked upon its transcendent power as it steamed from the vast depths below. There could be no higher purity, no greater *paramita* or perfection than this, expressing unfathomable nature here in the higher heights.

2003

DUSK ALONG THE MEKONG

LAOS

Laos isn't really on the way to anywhere else, and that has been its salvation. We'd had a slog journeying there, but by the time we found our lodgings in Vientiane, I'd got my mojo back. The Lao capital set along the Mekong still feels like a big village, and life moves slowly. Fifteen minutes' walk from town, our digs in an old French house, with an added section of eight or a dozen rooms, were never too busy. The lane out front of our lush tropical garden was overgrown with bougainvillea and frangipani blossoms, and only a bicycle or occasional *moto* might pass us, or a pair of monks in orange robes walking silently between the lane's bookend, gilded temples. Through shady pipal and magnolia shrubbery, we could see their beautifully tiled, dragon-curve roofs, ineffably relaxing to the eye. The Mekong chugged along unrelentingly down the way.

We'd arrived in moonlight, stopping at an ornate grill fence with an open gate and a friendly, not too loud, *"Sabaidee"* welcome at our guesthouse and grounds. Our room was large and airy with twelve-foot ceiling and fan—old-school Southeast Asia; furniture all solid teak. Nothing fancy, but spotlessly comfortable with a small pool to keep the body thermostat in check during the heat. We unpacked for the next four days, and Kwan-shik slipped outside. Minutes later she came back, our two compact travel thermoses in hand. "Hot water any time you like," she grinned, already reaching for her traveller's tea kit. "Kettle's in the morning room where there's breakfast. Sweet dreams."

Aging voyageurs come to endure certain indignities. You learn that discount tickets invariably mean hard seats on airplanes. More frequent visits to the lavatory oblige, well, ready access to a loo without need of a search party. Bruises take longer to heal, and stomach upset occurs regularly from unknown sources. Solution? Be mindful when packing your bathroom kit before departing; keep your Ibuprofen handy, pack that strip of Alka-Seltzers and those hand-sanitizers; buy mosquito wipes; and do not forget, as Long John Baldry reminds us in his "Everything Stops for Tea," a mini-kettle or thermos of boiling water goes a long way toward bringing contentment. If you can't buy this priceless portable hardware, at least bring the tea or instant coffee, whatever you cherish.

I'd wanted to see this small landlocked nation north of Thailand ever since receiving a postcard out of the blue from an editor friend. Like Cambodia and Vietnam, for a long time after the Indochina Wars in the mid-1970s, Laos had been closed to travellers while it worked at reimagining its new Communist political reality. Laos is the size of Britain with a population of barely seven million, mostly devout Theraveda Buddhists, and it borders five separate nations—Myanmar, Thailand, Vietnam, Cambodia, and China. Vientiane, the capital, has just over 700,000 souls and feels less than that. The morning rounds of orange-robed monks and novices as they file silently out of their temples to collect alms offerings of sticky rice, the national food, sets the tone for the day throughout the country. The card I'd received portrayed this daily *Tak Bat* ritual, emblematic of a state comprised chiefly of near-inaccessible mountain jungle, punctuated with tight river valleys. The 3,000-mile Mekong River winds out of the Tibetan Plateau to the distant northwest, and as it slopes down from Yunnan Province in China, it forms Laos's western border with Myanmar and its southern border with Thailand. Moving like a big, muddy python, it leads to the laid-back capital with its broad French-era boulevards, shady streets, open-air markets, and cozy Franco-colonial architecture that remains home to government ministries, foreign embassies, and the many NGOs here that work with Laos on an array of development projects. Roads, parks, medical and women's clinics, overpasses, educational projects, and so on are routinely completed with foreign help—many of them from quieter nations like Australia, Luxembourg, New Zealand. Germany, and South Korea. China and Japan find their way in too. Not a sign of Canada anywhere.

The French have long been present in Laos in one shade or another. Apart from the architecture in Vientiane, or the curious Arch de Triomphe in the downtown central area, though, you might wonder what they actually did during their century here. Tellingly, however, one notices a vestigial taste for vintage French wines that can turn up in the oddest little shops, and in the very good *patisseries* that turn up unexpectedly in locations where French nationals have fallen in love, married local, and carry on baking good bread, *croissants, flans,* what have you. *Vive la baguette!*

In search of cash our first morning, a call into an Australian NGO office that announced itself with a street sign seemed obvious. A quick introduction and a polite request for info is all it should take—get in and get out—"You want the morning market," a buxom Queenslander called from her desk. "Out the door, turn left, keep walking." And so we were pointed toward the best place imaginable. Good thing, since it turns up in few guidebooks. Bless the Downunders. A sprawling, outwardly chaotic-looking area, the morning market is anything but: Rather it's more an organic self-organizing principle of a thing with its own logic and is worth finding. The banks are there, because, well, the market is where the money is, right? Motorbike repair shops beside bakeshops, clothiers, jewellers, open-air barbeque stands, and fruit stalls. Turn off the main drag, and you're in a long cavern of cloth dealers—anything to do with fabric. Delightfully, no one seems out to cheat you on a price: There's some modest haggling if you fancy, but no wild veers up or down, and checking prices roundabout suggests these mostly women traders are honest dealers. At six or seven dollars, a heavy cotton, buttoned-up shirt will always come in handy. The traditional, elegant *sin* sarong patterns worn by women throughout Laos since ancient times come ready-made, or in bolts of dazzling, local-made quality.

Stopping for a fresh coconut to drain and munch—nothing better in the heat—we looked on from beneath the stand's sun umbrella as a mid-morning thumping, bumping fitness class pounded out the calories in a shaded courtyard across the street.

"Dancercise has reached Vientiane," a voice mused from behind us. "I saw you earlier; you're staying by the river, yes?"

And so it goes, a new acquaintance. "I'm from Switzerland," he said, offering his hand. "My name is Florent."

Europeans, we've found, are reserved by nature. They open up cautiously and typically don't go in much for swapping addresses. Florent, with a series of loopy body gestures and a steady smile was different. "Are you a martial arts guy?" I asked. "Yoga?"

"Don't laugh," he answered. "I'm a clown." And with that, he sagged like a Marcel Marceau mime. Then with a shake, he pulled himself straight again with a puppet-like finish. Not too shabby.

"Well done… I suppose you're going to tell us you ran away from a job as an accountant to join the circus?"

"Not exactly…" He'd been doing this a long time, he said. Fire-eating, juggling, acrobatics. We were walking together now, past the cloth stalls toward the entrance and the busyness of the street. "I fell in love with the romance of travel when I was a young guy. Now I'm still on the road with a European circus, and we tour a lot of the time—Africa, the Middle East, Scandinavia, Latin America. It's my little individual effort for world peace—making people laugh, having fun."

"Laos?"

"No, not working. I love it here and come back as often as I can. You've found yourselves a good spot away from the downtown. I stay in a little place behind where you're living. My girlfriend works close by."

"So you love this country, and a little bit of Laos has fallen in love with you?" Kwan-shik asked. Florent grinned, arms akimbo again.

"Could be! Do you like some coffee? There's a good place not too far walking from here. I'll show you. Laos has great coffee—they grow it down south on the Bolaven Plateau. It's the long eastern arm of territory reaching toward Cambodia. My girlfriend showed me the region. The Mekong grows very wide there and is full of lovely islands, hundreds of them."

"That's south of the old Ho Chi Minh Trail?"

"Exactly, or one good part of it. The trail shadowed the frontier with Vietnam all the way to Cambodia."

We set off, following Florent as he demystified Lao cultural ins and outs for us. "Downtown Vientiane is very *laissez-faire*, but restaurants and bars close around 10:30 or 11 PM to deflect the Bangkok party-town syndrome that has metastasized through Southeast Asia," he said. "After a trial period when the country opened up and the yahoos poured in to drink and swing and raise hell the way they'd learned in Thailand, the government decided against goofball tourism. One thing about communism: it can get results in a hurry." He snapped his fingers. "Done."

"People aren't crazy here though," Florent continued. "A few streets away from the centre downtown, you'll still see street-corner noodle stands dishing up bowls to late-night workers and the properly hungry. It's common sense."

Kwan-shik asked Florent about regular boiling water at guesthouses in Laos. "Probably, if you ask. That's Laos. Ask and you shall usually receive, but the water they give you will be safe. They are a clean people. I never get sick in this country."

He pointed to a dark wood-framed café, and we took a table in the shade out front. Vientiane is a low-rise city, only rarely do buildings rise higher than three stories—one of the last of the region's sweet-spot cities. Businesses offer most services you might need, and plenty of guesthouses of all sizes offer accommodation of one sort or another, according to the government newspaper, the *Vientiane Times* that publishes in English daily. It's not a bad read unless you crave celebrity or Western political gossip of which you'll find *nil.*

"There's so little official presence visible in the streets," I remarked.

"This is not China," Florent motioned with a shake of his curly hair. "What does Chuang-tzu the Taoist say? 'Govern the people as you would cook a small fish, *Lightly.*'" Raising his iced-coffee that had arrived, he set his face cheerfully. "*Ciao amigos.*"

Within a few days, we met a number of foreigners who've chosen to call Laos home.

"Wonderful spot," a graying Canadian from Thunder Bay shared as we stood inquiring about rates for therapeutic massage. "You wonder what might have developed if these gracious Southeast Asian people had just been left alone instead of that long war."

"This place any good?" I asked.

"It's hard to beat," Carl replied. "Under ten dollars for an hour of deep tissue work in clean premises. I come here with my wife. Tell them just how you prefer it. You want soft, no problem. You want strong, tell 'em: They'll have someone who was working in the rice fields a month ago, with hands like a blacksmith."

Apart from the President's mansion, worth a look through the gates, there's not a lot else especially noteworthy en route along the river. You pass the enormous new hospital being built by the Chinese, with a separate building reserved for their own workers, part of China's "Belt Road Initiative" drawing the world inexorably toward Zhong Guo, the old Middle Kingdom. As the promotional maxim has it, "One Belt, One Road." For the Laos, Kazakhs, Africans, and the like, they get roads and clinics while China gets to export its over-capacity of production, and of raw Chinese labour especially. Recently, 10,000 Chinese workers have been building new rail lines in Thailand. As a grand strategy under President Xi Jinping, it is masterful in softly asserting Chinese behaviour over its neighbour states; for as China's influence waxes ever more dynamically, it becomes a rule maker, not taker. Its ability to pressure neighbouring states like Laos with punitive economic measures keeps growing. We'd shortly see blunt evidence of this upcountry. Meanwhile, China continues with a new railway line direct to Tibet, and the China-Pakistan Railway is driving through some of the world's most dramatic mountain ranges, not to mention the 21st century's new Maritime Silk Road. That's a lot of building. The price of this "alternative to globalization," as the Chinese see it? US $224 billion. Say what you like about the mandarins in Beijing, but they demonstrate a cohesive vision of leadership in stark contrast to the West's groaning lack of direction during the past twenty years.

Afternoons are a good time to meander the shady side lanes of downtown with their cafés and bookshops. You can find an outdoor restaurant offering big beers on sale and settle in for what soon starts looking like your own main meal of the day, not too unlike the monks that eat early, then fast until next morning. Lao dishes are not as fiery as Thai, pleasing to the eye and taste buds, and pungent with fresh pounded ginger, lemongrass, garlic, and fish sauce. Beef salads are superb; tofu is served in ingenious combinations for vegetarians, and the sticky rice and fresh mango for dessert is out-of-this-world good.

You can walk Vientiane in a couple of days. It's an awfully dusty place come dry season though, in what's a nasty greater East Asian phenomenon. Annually now, a great cloud of fine particles from the Gobi Desert and unknown northern parts begins settling ever more frequently over cities here, mingling with urban pollution in creating a thick smog-soup. Do your lungs need this? Nor is this a new thing: A thousand years ago, China's brilliant Tang and Sung dynasty poets harked in their writing to "the red dust of the world"—think of arid Xian, the old capital, with its 200-strong dromedary camel trading caravans farting their way through the dust. Life doesn't change much even in the 21st century once the winds and diesel lorries stir up the mix; so with homage to Tu Fu, Li Bai, Baijuyi, and the other poetic ancients, after resting a few days in low-key, comfortable Vientiane, we skipped town early.

In Luang Prabang, the old spiritual capital, there's an overpoweringly lovely mix of stupendous Buddhist temples with the remaining colonial hotel-villas along the Mekong, and a few modern buildings going here and there, but none permitted over two storeys. Always there's the lazy Mekong River nearby.

Road life isn't always rosy. What looks a good bet online for lodging can be disappointing on arrival—gloomy back lane locations, lack of air, low ceilings inviting sudden knockouts, steep steps, surly staff. We've decided it's just as well to eat a night's cost and start looking for a new spot right away. Luang Prabang is a peninsula situated at the confluence of the Mekong and smaller Nam Khan rivers. A better class of place at a better rate usually turns up quickly. A cold glass of fresh juice while you unpack is fairly customary here, and a wash and cool down in a horizontal position will get you ready for the world again. You can walk up to the main drag, Thanon Sakkarin. A first look at the main stretch can be, uhm, not what you'd expect. Young backpackers roam up and down the road that's fronted all the way at ground level with shop fronts—trinket shops stand cheek by jowl with restaurants, adventure trek and river excursion ticket outlets, clothing boutiques. It's the same scene you've come across in Thailand, Nepal, Guatemala, Haida Gwaii, Bali... the flip side of ecotourism. But take a deep breath: The food is good and inexpensive, the big cold bottles of Beerlao will settle your nerves, and in the dry season, the weather is fine—warm by day, cool at night. Residential houses are tucked in along the overgrown side streets with the town's thirty-three Buddhist temples, and tropical blooms fall wiggly-waggly over bamboo fences fronting property lines of all shapes and sizes. You can amble among the lanes and nobody minds. Guesthouses are woven into the local housing tapestry, and few corners will be without a decent place to eat. Young dogs snuffle and play, and always in the background, there's the steady tonal chatter of Lao from somewhere in a terrace garden or from a screened balcony. Life goes on.

Luang Prabang is a former royal capital, small and slower, and nearer the great wild northern mountain jungles that border southern China's Yunnan province. A town of 25,000, it is full of spectacular Buddhist temples. Our last morning, we rose at 5:30 AM to attend the daily *Tak Bak* ritual. It's a symbiotic arrangement; they support each other for all the right reasons. The sun rises by six AM, illuminating the landscape of misty sudden mountains, and the Mekong River wandering by is entrancing. The whole town is a natural walkabout, a UNESCO World Heritage Site for its living religious architecture.

Two days previous, we had taken a riverboat three hours northeast of town amidst endless mountain realms of teak forest that run direct to shore, punctuated by subsistence agriculture plots that grow an astonishing range of vegetable crops. In dry season, the river allows these marginal, narrow floodplain holdings on an impermanent basis and small farmers grow table greens, pineapple, cauliflower and broccoli, garlic, runner beans, onion and scallions, corn, carrots, numerous squash and marrow varieties, sugarcane, and fruit of wonderful abundance—papayas all year-round, crisp apples, small apple bananas, watermelon, dragon fruit, and oranges. The Lao are mainly fish eaters, although there's chewy fowl, pork, and water buffalo available. The river journey was entrancing, a National Geographic Society sort of experience.

The Mekong is the raison d'être for the whole show. Long riverboats, narrow in beam with raised poop deck at back, cut upriver with their motors, and you pass an amazing sight at the confluence of the mother snake and its younger tributary, the Nam Khan, where its livelier waters join into the tireless downstream flow. One fisherman lolls midstream, pulling at a handline. Boats appear and disappear, the water always busy. On the farther bank of the river, a small rash of houses emerges from the bush, then a temple higher up the slope.

"What a dreamy landscape," Kwan-shik murmured. "Like an opium poem."

You move through this vast territory of the river of life and death—small villages here and there, waterfront farm clearings, lumber scows tied up along shore, then a jail with watchtowers like something out of *The Bridge on the River Kwai*. I asked the one boatman that could speak some English, "What's happening?"

"Jail for northern province..."

That's it? Large enough perhaps for a couple of hundred inmates. It's a low-crime country for starters. Gleaming white buildings, green roofs. Back on the river, a detritus of plastic bottles and junk dots the river surface, a quiet disappointment. Another humble country brought to this. Then farther on again, and we passed the elephant loggers, with the great beasts hauling logs and carts up dusty trails to and from the river. "Lord, look at the size of them..."

At a newer village with a temple, indicating they're Lao or Khmer, the boat pulls in and you skip over the bamboo catwalk to shore. There's a small cloth bazaar, and it takes some patience to escape the entreaties of the women selling their wares. Onward a little, there's some space, and a young girl weaves at her loom. It's like a scene from the Middle Ages. The exquisite fabrics you've seen in town or down the path are made in cottage operations like this: the girl looks up and invites us to sample her stock. Why not? My grandmother was a Yorkshire weaver by trade, uncles and aunts as well at Bradford's mighty Lister's Mill, and in the carpet weaving at Tong. With a natural sympathy for this timeless work, I watched almost in a trance as the lovely young woman held her thread of weft yarn, weaving and passing her shuttle back and forth, grooming in the warp thread, weaving in the weft.

"She's casting a spell on you,' Kwan-shik nudged. "We ought to buy something here. She makes the most beautiful cloth I've ever laid eyes on, and nothing costs very much to begin with."

Not long ago, these were the opium villagers of the northern hills. Now, new incentive projects have them growing quality coffee beans and weaving for the eco-tourism trade. By all accounts, they are proving reasonably successful, and you can't help but feel good for the locals. The tribal poor never did get much besides heavy weapons and the most sordid kinds of trafficking for their efforts from the bad guys anyway. And it's a women's enterprise to boot: more power to them. An extraordinary moment along the trail, not soon forgotten.

Heading back to the river, a couple of Europeans asked if we'd show them what we'd bought. They'd been too nervous, they said, to bring out their cash beyond the town. What cultural timidity!

On the river again, we chugged on further into the bush. Scanning the shoreline for birds with my binoculars, incongruously I caught sight of what appeared to be a massive concrete footing. *Here?* In the middle of… where were we exactly? We chugged on, passing a herd of water buffalo, more elephants, bird life. The concrete heap grew larger; then a line of them hove into view before disappearing into the bush. I asked the boatman about the pallisters.

"China-Laos Railway," he replied. "All way from Beijing to Singapore… We don't like." He gestured with his hand. "Too much China in Laos. We have map." He turned and rooted through some papers in the galley. There it was, all 414 kilometres of it, north-south from Yunnan to Vientiane, then south into Thailand, Malaysia, and on to the Heart of the Dragon, Singapore. Expected completion, 2021. *Gulp, soon come!* Thirty stations will mark the route from China to Vientiane, more than forty percent of which will be tunnelled, some up to three kilometers in length. At present there are perhaps four or five legitimate town-stops in Laos. Much of the behemoth will be elevated to deal with rugged terrain, ravines, and rivers. Those new stops will be fertile points for outward expansion east and west: what that means for the teak forest is a deeply limited future. Mining will quickly follow. We know who'll handle the labour.

We hired a guide next day and planned on trekking eight or ten hours toward some Hmong hamlets in the hills. Phivan was a knowledgeable young Lao, and he brought along a point-man pal who unfailingly brought up the rear, a Hmong with ability in several other hill tongues. We set off after our lift dropped us off north near the shores of the Nam Khan. Crossing a long bamboo bridge, we followed country trails, quiet and not yet hot. Along the shore, a father and son cast their fishnets. Phivan, our guide, pointed out dark clumps of river weed, the dried laver that goes in soup and noodle dishes.

"Where did you learn your English?"

"At school. When I was a boy, we lived on a farm near the forest. Then my parents passed away. I was raised by SOS."

Kwan-shik and I exchanged a look. SOS is the world's largest children's aid charitable organization. Those adverts you see on late-night television? Here, one of those grown-up kids was leading us through the northern Lao forest as capably as a young professor. It's unlikely he earned a lot as a guide, but surely more than others working in cafés or driving a *tuk-tuk* all day. We ambled along past pineapple fields cut into hillsides above the trail. Papaya and other fruit groves were in various states of growth—rambutans, longan, thick shady tamarinds.

"Most of the villages here grow one kind of food; they sell it in Luang Prabang," Phivan notes, bushwhacking ahead with a dry length of bamboo. He'd lived on tapioca when his parents died, he said, too poor for rice. Manioc, cassava, tapioca, sago—the basic belly-filling starch of the poor in the world's tropical zones. You see pictures of the malnourished kids with tapioca bellies. For the lucky affluent like us, it's an occasional delicious dessert with cream and sugar.

Hour after hour, we marched north, stopping to look at wild plants, eating them—some sweet, others bitter—learning about them, occasionally passing *swidden* farm plots burned from out of the hillside forest—Asia's timeless semi-nomadic, upland agricultural tradition. "A small field lasts five years, then the soil is used up," Phivan noted. The nutrients leach out faster than buffalo dung, and ash can renew the soil. He knew much of the local flora and fauna, of tribal customs, and he spoke the best English we'd yet heard here. In dense bush, he indicated near-invisible bird traps set by tribals; pointing upwards, he traced the equally near-invisible filament cloud nets also used to capture birds in flight. Every hour or so in a clearing, we'd pass small fat cattle with shiny coats, or a small goat herd chomping at the underbrush. Cutting hard up a slope beneath a tall forest canopy, we noticed the stink first, a raw raunchy crud that got in your nostrils: "rubber plantation."

This wasn't the sort of tidy plantation from British Malaya that gave the world its first automobile tires. Rubber trees grow for thirty years, tapped in the dry season; the rains make the latex too runny otherwise. The trees are not so big around and are grown in approximately linear formations in squares hacked out of the native teak forest. Each has its small can to collect the latex sap, and the sour stench is rotten. "Rich people own these forest plantations," Phivan nodded, pointing through the trees. "The tappers—the people who live in those shacks—they get to stay here where they work."

"Like sharecropper life in Mississippi's blues delta," I said to Kwan-shik.

"During the war, we used to hear about the Pathet Lao, the guerilla fighters. Did they ever operate out here?"

Phivan scanned the territory around us. "All this was Pathet Lao." The old war zone.

Moving on above a stiff ravine and bamboo grove, we caught sight of an elephant-shaped mountain. The jaggedy parts of the peak were *karst,* limestone, Phivan explained. It gets eaten by the rain and weather. Then another form of agri-architecture claimed the horizon, stretching off to the distance. "Palm oil groves," Phivan said, waving his cane.

"One of the tropical rainforest's greatest enemies," I said. "They've burned off Borneo and swaths of the South Pacific for it… Palm oil goes in everything: soap, biscuits, biodiesel, shampoo." We stopped a moment to catch our breath on the incline. Across a dusty track, pickup trucks rumbled in and out; a rough wooden storage canopy covered a woodpile.

"The palm trees are not so old," Phivan indicated. The covered wood is teak, cut down, and just left heaped there. This was the old forest. Someone had been up here with a small one-man sawmill cutting the precious hardwood. Any single rough plank would have been worth $100 or more back home to a decent boat builder for setting on a lathe and crafting fine woodwork. Piles of aging timber dotted the undergrowth. Palm oil got the attention.

The trek was brilliant, perhaps no more than fifteen miles to the north all in, but the hillside trails grew stiffer and the drops into steep ravines more obvious. Dense, dry jungle bush everywhere. Phivan stopped to pluck soft, purple blossoms, stashing some in his pack. "These we call 'Hmong flowers,' very pretty." They were. "We call them *kiloa*. You can boil the roots to stop diarrhoea immediately. The leaves heal cuts."

An hour and a half on, sweating and puffing on our walking sticks we'd each acquired along the trail, we entered a dusty settlement of bamboo huts, storage shacks raised on stilts, perhaps twenty or thirty families. Roosters pursued chickens, tiny chicks raced for cover, ducks squawked around a damp water patch, dogs panted in the shade of houses. Decades back we'd seen hill-tribe villages in northern Thailand; that had been a Neolithic encounter up close. The only thing that had changed here, I noted, were the corrugated tin roofs in view. Still a stark subsistence living, but with some modest sort of progress. We passed a large weaving hut; half a dozen older women worked on a long run of fabric filigreed with metallic-like tinsel designs. A younger woman suckled her baby; they watched us pass by with no compelling interest in our presence.

"Is this a Hmong village?" Kwan-shik asked. She'd been mulling on a distant kinship query involving her own people's origins.

"Yes."

The ten percent of Laotian peoples known as the *Lao Soung*, or highlanders, live at greater than 1,000 feet above sea level, and they include a diverse spread of minority tribal cultures indigenous to the isolated north. The term "Hmong" usually refers to these tribal groups of Tibeto-Burman linguistic origin, and unfortunately they continue to have public relations issues with many Laotians. It's a situation replicated among Indigenous tribals around the world. An animistic array of peoples with pantheistic beliefs in the spirits of the land, water, and natural world, this can place them at some odds with the country's conventional Theraveda Buddhist majority. The barely educated and economically undeveloped Hmong were extensively recruited as mercenaries by the Americans during the hellish Indochina wars of the 1960s and 70s, and it was their misfortune to end up on the losing side of history. Many were forced to flee into remote northern Thailand, or endure "reeducation" in prison camps. In some regions, hard feeling and resistance continue.

Time for a break. We stopped at a large woven bamboo hut with a lattice fence around it. A heavy teak plank table rested in a dusty yard between several outbuildings and the main dwelling. Guinea fowl scurried from us, a pair of nondescript dogs shifted from beneath the table and slumped beneath a raised wooden tray growing what looked like salad greens; a young women with a baby disappeared inside the hut. Phivan spoke through his sideman to an older fellow who passed the woman and may have been her husband; he was clearly the headman.

"You can wash your hands back there," Phivan said. "There is a well."

Indeed a public well had been driven deep nearby—a reliable source of clean water, and a rare something for the people. That wasn't all. Further away, the hill people now had a public loo with two squat holes above a concrete septic drainage. I washed my hands and rinsed my head and neck. Phivan joined me. "This is from the UN," he said matter-of-factly.

The simple contribution from someone or other's honourable project was worthy of thanks. Presumably there'd be children here that might not die young as a result. Inchworm progress on behalf of our common humanity. Amen. I thought, finally an actual sign that the UN really does do something besides host conferences.

Back at the table, contemplating the bamboo container of sticky rice and a small plate of fried, chopped greens that an older woman brought to us, I pulled out my harmonica and played a few Canuck folk tunes. Instantly, half a dozen kids came running, gawking, then swaying about giddy with the music. It was almost an SOS late-night fundraising moment: only a heart of stone wouldn't want to help these people who had so little. Phivan would spread a little cash around for the simple meal.

So we made merry before eating, yet not without a little trepidation on our part: I thought of the Europeans who'd been afraid to trade with the locals on the river and felt a bit miserable about my reticence to eat. But the rice was good, a bit dry, and the greens were warm.

"Is there a school here?" Kwan-shik asked.

"Yes, one teacher..."

"One for the whole village?"

"Yes, teacher let these boys come to see you." We wondered where the girls were.

Then we were off again, sticking to drinking water from our own bottles, just in case. Toward the end of the dusty village, in which few people moved about but were surely aware of our presence, the sandy trail widened into what looked like a rough truck track. At the very edge of the settlement, a shack was open. "Shop," said Phivan. We had a look. Empty shelves; a few packets of candy, some single-use packets of soap, and what must have been Aspirin; a few simple notebooks for school and a cluster of pencils. There wasn't a single thing we could purchase. I asked about a few plastic bags of clear fluid—"What's that?"

"*Lao-lao*... happy water." You might need a drink after a rough day around here, for sure.

Someone or other pulled up here in a vehicle from time to time, that much was clear. Cheerfully, it made the walking easier. "Be careful!" Phivan called, pointing his cane in the air. "Wasp nest!" Reflexively we looked upward. A gigantic grey paper hive hung well above our heads in a type of redwood. We moved faster. A hundred yards along, a cultivated field organized with poles and bamboo crossbeams. "Beans and hops!" Phivan called back to us.

I asked about the rough road we were following. "The government gets the hill people to move in closer so they can have a school and be closer to a road. They can sell something in town that they grow, or wood to make charcoal. And they have safe water."

The Luddite in me wondered how good that was for the Hmong. Phivan may have seen my quandary. "I have been fortunate," he said. "I got education and learned English, and today I'm meeting you and your wife. I get to work. In Luang Prabang, I live in a room, and I can cook outside. I have a young dog that is so much fun for my younger sister and me. Look!" He pulled out a cell phone and showed us a photograph of a small crowded room and a puppy, then a small fenced yard. "I grow some of our food—I know how. I look after my two younger brothers. I learn English from TV and YouTube. My old English teacher from SOS, he wants me to come and work for him; he will start a tour guide company. And I have a girlfriend. She is seventeen. All this is good."

"Not yet twenty and you look after yourself, two brothers, and a sister. And probably soon to get married." Kwan-shik smiled. Phivan practically blushed with pleasure. Then he squatted in the clearing—"Look!"; a thick draggy smudge scuffed the dusty trail.

"What's that?"

"Python, like anaconda. He pass by just a while ago. Big one. Let's go…" With another shake of head, Kwan-shik observed that the school kids were less than half a mile from where we stood. "It's a tough neighbourhood."

The next two hours sloped downhill, and we followed along, numbed and damp with the heat. Then we sensed the change in the air and caught a first glimpse of a cobbled river bar. Shortly, we gallumped down a stiff trail that elephants might have used, worn and rutted. Phivan hooted and waved to a couple of fishermen across the river. We waited in the shade watching the young fast flow of water, cooling ourselves off with hatfuls of cold showery wet. Ten minutes later, the gas-burning roar of a long-tail motor came around a bend, and one of the fishers angled toward a footing and we scrambled aboard.

"Take off your packs!" Phivan hollered. "Get them off!" If you fall in, they weigh you down and you drown. It's very cold!"

He was correct, but the cold felt welcome on our heads and neck. The long-tail boat cut around, and we set off downriver. For thirty minutes, we surged past dense forest until a village stood out in a clearing on our left. We jumped clear, wet with foam from the shallow boat, getting only partly wet as we splashed for land. Phivan squared up with the boatman, and we marched up the riverbank to where a simple market of fruit and vegetable shacks stood at the edge of a shade tree canopy.

For another half hour, we aired our tired feet and munched watermelon and chunks of ambrosial pineapple. The driver who had let us off that morning wheeled in, and we hauled aboard back for town. Incongruously, a flatbed truck pulled ahead of us ferrying a life-size gold Buddha image, presumably for a temple, and we followed it respectfully.

Twenty-five minutes out from Luang Prabang, Phivan yelled to us in the back—"*Gang-Noon* is that way," nosing to the river.

"Gang-Noon?"

"Monsieur Henri Mouhot is buried there. You can see the place of his memorial. He discovered Angkor Wat in Cambodia when France was here."

Henri Mouhot? In the late 1850s, Mouhot embarked on a series of expeditions in Siam, Cambodia, and Laos with sponsorship from the Royal Geographical Society and the Zoological Society of London when the French government rejected his scientific overtures. As a botanist, ornithologist, and entomologist, he and his research findings were highly respected and several species of insects and spiders are named in his honour. In 1860 in northern Cambodia, he encountered the centuries-long abandoned temples and ruins of the vast Angkor Wat complex that had been the centre of one of the world's great but historically neglected empires. Incorrectly, but well intended, he has since been credited with "discovering" Angkor Wat. But the sprawling complex of thirty-nine temples at Angkor had never been lost, simply ignored by time and had returned to a state of nature, overgrown with towering banyan trees that spread their great thick roots over everything in their wake, dismantling whole temples. Mouhot died of malaria fever the following year near Luang Prabang. His resting place beside the Nam Khan was overgrown and forgotten until 1989, when it too was "rediscovered" and cleared from the jungle. Mouhot's posthumously published accounts of his adventures directly inspired the restoration work that has gone into the Angkor complex. Woefully, Angkor became the stronghold of the Khmer Rouge whose grotesque social revolution resulted in the deaths of 1.3 million Cambodians during the Killing Fields period after the Vietnam/Indochina Wars, and the last of those psychopaths held out at Angkor until 1998. By contrast, Mouhot's humility and adventurous spirit survive, and his burial place remains a shrine for deep trekkers.

A last dusky evening in Luang Prabang needs spending by the Mekong. We found a table at a restaurant platform on a slope above the river with the light beginning to fall and the mist settling over the sleepy dragon peaks. The Mekong flowed muddy green into a lazy bend downstream, and below us the rough-tilled garden slopes were verdant with papaya and bananas. From a temple across the road, the evening chanting of the monks and novices resonated through a grove, as we gazed upon a stretch of the river with a few lantern boats setting out to fish, and the mountains and the mist at their most breathtaking. "I think it's the loveliest spot on Earth," I told Kwan-shik, "but I've said that before, elsewhere…"

From the tiny storytelling theatre nearby, an old farmer wheezed into his *khaene,* the vertical bamboo mouth organ of the hill people. We mused upon the joys and bumps of travel, and on the crazy, haunting music of the bamboo pipes that are so much of this place. Earlier that afternoon, we'd released some fish into the river, a small act of atonement among Buddhists here. We had much to be thankful for, and me at least, a few sins in need of forgiveness. In this quiet bliss at the end of day beneath a dimming apricot sky, life was like a dream, a peaceful world. It came to me that a good death must be like this.

The full-on brunt of globalization hasn't fully hit Laos yet, but you can sense it's on the way. From a spiritual perspective, that's unsettling. Yet economics devotees will always cheer the other side, with some justification—Phivan and his little family band are examples. Modernization isn't a blanket reality; there's good and bad aplenty out in the world. Choose mindfully. On our way to East Asia, we'd stopped a few nights in Seoul on family and sentimental errands. Our second day, we stopped during a long afternoon hike at an inspiring ecological site. Amidst high-rise towers and crowded avenues, the ancient stream at Cheonggyecheon that had flowed through the city in earlier days has returned to life. Kwan-shik remembered it as the cloth-dyers district where squatters' shanties poured filth into a sluggish stream. Now it has been reclaimed, although the city expands far beyond. Imagine in the beating heart of a modern metropolis that a lovely flowing stream with burbling waterfalls, wild marsh grass, and native bushes can still go about its business and flourish. Residents can stroll or sit and contemplate along the sides of this compact natural jewel. More amazing, near a small bridge a tall grey heron waded in the shadows; it hopped then struck, taking silvery wriggling fish. How did it get here? The heron's elegant black head chevron was radiant against its long white neck and subtle grey-green plumage. How could such a blessing coexist within the clamour and congestion of 21st century urban life? It happened purely because enough citizens believed in its importance. If we just give things a chance...

So, the joys and bumps of travel: the crazy music of what happens. Better to make up our own mind. There's nothing like seeing things full in the face—pristine wilderness and the razor-gash of material progress. It's the new colonialism for our global century. But as the Sung dynasty poet Su Tung-Po has it, "The sound of the valley stream is itself the Vast Eternal Tongue." Ask the explorers or your granny what's really important. Ask the Lao. May every sincere traveller be blessed with the sublime gifts of longevity, good health, great happiness, and wisdom.

Sabaidee...

2020

Hemingway's Corner Table - Cojimar, Cuba

ACKNOWLEDGEMENTS

For earlier versions of some of these stories, the author thanks: *subTerrain; Pacific Rim Review of Books; Common Ground; Kyoto Journal; Shambhala Sun; Arts Alive; Shared Vision; Return to Stillness: Twenty Years with a Tai Chi Master; The Pillow Book of Dr Jazz; The Summer Book.*

My historical knowledge of California was helped by reading *From West to East: California and the Making of the American Mind* by Stephen Schwartz (The Free Press, 1998).

The epigraph by Patricia Monaghan is from *The Red-Haired Girl from the Bog: The Landscape of Celtic Myth and Spirit* (New World Library, 2004).

The author also expressly thanks the following for their support and encouragement:
Mona Fertig, Peter Haase, Laura Andrés Tallardà, Dr. Nicholas Kats, Brian Kaufman, Michelle Pahl, Glenys Welters, Sam Sen Gupta, Uma Mitra, Eugenia Stojka, Vincent Varga, Piotr Dejneka, Roman Ejryszew, Alan Twigg, the Liddy family, Dolores Carolan, Joseph Roberts, Leza Lowitz, Perrine Angly, Rex Weyler, Pearl Luke, Paul Falardeau, Charlotte Franson, Mother Tongue Publishing's team, and as ever, Kwan-shik Kwon.

Photo: Mike Wakefield

ABOUT THE AUTHOR

Trevor Carolan began writing as a backpacking reporter for *The Columbian* newspaper while in high school in 1968 and has since visited more than 50 countries. His work includes many books of non-fiction, poetry, and anthologies. He has held a number of senior arts appointments during his career, and was elected municipal councillor in North Vancouver following campaigns on behalf of Indigenous land claims and watershed conservation issues. He received a PhD in International Relations from Bond University, Queensland, for studies in Literature, Ecology, and Ideas of the Sacred in the Global Age. His documentary film *Cascadia: The Life and Breath of the World* features many distinguished writers and is based on his co-edited Eco-Lit collection of the same title which received a Best American Essays Citation in 2013. His books include *Giving Up Poetry: With Allen Ginsberg at Hollyhock; Return to Stillness: Twenty Years with a Tai Chi Master; The Literary Storefront: The Glory Years, Vancouver's Literary Centre 1978-1985; In Formless Circumstance: Poems from the Road & Home;* and *New World Dharma: Encounters with Buddhist Teachers, Writers, and Leaders.* The long-time International Editor of *Pacific Rim Review of Books,* Carolan reads internationally, frequently with musicians, and is Professor Emeritus at University of the Fraser Valley. More at trevorcarolan.com.

Trevor and Kwan-Shik atop Phu Si hill, Luang Prabang, Laos

Along the Mekong, Laos